TWO

CULTURES

ONE

MARRIAGE

Premarital Counseling
for Mixed Marriages

TWO

CULTURES

ONE

MARRIAGE

Premarital Counseling
for Mixed Marriages

Reger C. Smith, Ph.D.

ANDREWS UNIVERSITY PRESS
BERRIEN SPRINGS, MICHIGAN

I am grateful to the many partners in mixed marriages whose experiences directly and indirectly inspired and provided material for this effort.

Special gratefulness is felt toward my wife Katherine for being consistently supportive and for putting up with the clutter of manuscript copies.

Andrews University Press
Berrien Springs, MI 49104-1700
616-471-6915
FAX 616-471-6224

©1996 Andrews University Press

ISBN 1-883925-07-X
Library of Congress Catalog Card Number: 96-083149

Printed in the United States of America
99 98 97 96   5 4 3 2 1

Contents

Preface

T his short volume will not cover comprehensively the subject of intergroup marriage. Chapter 2 looks at some racial groups in the United States that may become involved in intermarriage. Chapter 3 covers some of the dynamics and relationship characteristics that can result from the merging in marriage of diverse cultures. Chapter 4 is devoted to a viewpoint of the Bible's teachings on interfaith and interreligious marriages, the positions of several Christian denominations on interdenominational and interfaith marriages, and the discussion of some problems of interreligious marriages. Chapter 5 deals with some of the concerns about the fate of children of mixed marriages. Chapter 6 describes some of the personal characteristics and skills that can enhance the success of a cross-cultural counselor. And Chapter 7 gives some suggestions for formats, content, and methodology in mixed-marriage counseling. I conducted some in-depth interviews with a small number of mixed-couple partners. Some of their foresight, their hindsight, and their current experiences in interracial marriage are referred to from time to time throughout the book.

A Social Systems Approach

While it is not always explicit or even apparent, a social systems framework as a basic way of understanding human relationships undergirds this book. This approach takes into account the various social systems the counselee(s) belongs or relates to. It traces the input-output exchanges among the relevant systems and notes how the various systems maintain their boundaries.

The family is best understood as a living system, composed of members who do not function independently of one another but as a unified whole. The family is a subsystem of the extended family which is a subsystem of one or more ethnic groups (religious, language, national, racial).

The book cites examples of black-white marriages more than any other mixture. This is because (1) there are more such marriages, (2) there is more concern in the United States about such marriages and more is written about them, and (3) United States society can be divided into "minorities" and "dominant society." The minorities share, to a greater or lesser extent, some of the consequences of prejudice and a lower social position. Therefore, much of the discussion on black-white marriages is generalizable to other mixed marriages. I hope that the reader can make the translations wherever suitable.

A basic assumption that directs the focus of this book is that, in most instances, the premarital counselor of a transracial couple will be white and belong to the dominant society.

I

Social and Historical Setting: It Happens

A Caucasian woman planning to marry a Korean comes to you for counseling; your best friend (white) is dating a black person; or your favorite cousin (Hispanic) just got engaged to a red-headed Irishman. If you are a counselor, you may be concerned about helping to sort out the complex factors involved. If you are a friend or a relative, you may experience a disturbing mixture of emotions and fears—what will other relatives think? Will the racial difference prevent a happy marriage? And what about the children?

This book primarily is concerned with mixed marriages in the United States because interracial problems here have few parallels elsewhere in the world. The number of interracial marriages in this country will continue to increase as members of different races meet and socialize more and more as equals in schools, churches, recreational programs, and at work.

Attitudes about racial intermarriage are shaped by history and the current status of race relations. In America, the "melting-pot," a number of racial groups have not blended in smoothly. In general, the greater the perceived differences between any one of these groups and the dominant racial group, the greater the prejudice and discrimination that group has experienced. Such differences can be in background, geographical factors, appearance, culture, and economics. Of course, such differences are demonstrated most clearly by the past and present situation of African-Americans in the United States. Because of the size of the black population, black-white marriage is the most common form of intermarriage. It is also the mixture that arouses

1

the most fears and the greatest resentment. Such unions were once illegal in many states—a situation based on the history of blacks as slaves and, later, as legally defined second-class citizens.

The 1967 opinion written by Justice Earl Warren of the United States Supreme Court signaled the end of miscegenation (mixed race marriage) laws in the few states that still observed them at that time. Within the next 15 years, the number of interracial marriages in the United States more than doubled (Wilson 1984, 34).

Currently, black-white marriages are the most common of interracial marriages, and, recently, they have increased the most. *Essence* magazine reported that in 1983, 164,000 (more than half) of the existing interracial marriages were black-white (Norment 1985, 156). Hawaii, Alaska, and California report the highest rates of interracial marriages. The large numbers of Japanese, Chinese, and Koreans who live in these states intermarry with Caucasians much more frequently than other minority groups (Kitano et al. 1984, 179). Although interracial marriages are more common now than ever before, they still do not comprise more than 2% of all marriages in the United States. Interfaith and interreligious marriages also are increasing (Glenn 1982, 156).

Although the percentage of black-white marriages compared to the total number of marriages in the United States remains small, some recent trends are noteworthy. The number of white-male/black-female unions (heretofore no more than 10% of black-white marriages) increased 20% from 1980 to 1987 (Randolph 1989, 156). Included in this count are a number of well-known entertainers. Another interesting trend is the number of interracial romances in recent movies and current television shows.

Interracial marriage rates among most other minorities are considerably higher than for blacks. For example, 40.6% of Japanese American women and 53.7% of Native American women marry men outside of their group (Tucker & Mitchell-Kernan 1990, 209).

Let's Speak the Same Language

Perhaps it will be helpful to define some of the terms being used in this book. Some of these words are often misunderstood, and some wrongly are used interchangeably. These definitions will help make the book readily useful to persons who may have limited background in the behavioral sciences.

Acculturation—When groups of persons with different shared cultural meanings come into contact, the dominant group effects changes on the approaching group. These changes are a dynamic process of selective adaptation of the values, roles, and personality factors of the dominant group by the approaching group.

Culture—Culture includes knowledge, beliefs, art, morals, laws, customs, behaviors, feelings, attitudes, and any other habits and capabilities learned by human beings as members of society. Culture is learned and none of it is inherited. (It is not "in the genes" or passed down through "the blood.") It is not synonymous with race. Two people of the same race can have different cultural backgrounds and people from two different races can share the same cultural background.

Discrimination—Discrimination is overt behavior (actions) in which members of a group are treated unfavorably on the basis of their religious, cultural, or racial membership. It is usually based on an attitude of prejudice, but a person can discriminate without being prejudiced. An individual or a group can mistreat another individual or member of another group because of ignorance or societal pressure *without the person mistreating feeling negative or mean toward the person or persons being mistreated.*

Ethnic group—An ethnic group begins with a sense of identity and belonging based on loyalty to a distinctive cultural pattern related to common ancestry, religion, and/or race. It is a group, or subculture (see below), that has a common cultural tradition. Members may be geographically separated and yet remain aware that they belong to the group.

Homogamy—Homogamy refers to the similarities of partners who marry each other. Most marriages are homogamous—within race, within ethnic group, and/or within religion. Individuals tend to choose mates who are like them physically, psychologically, and socially.

Institutional racism—Institutional racism is the condition in which people of one racial group are systematically oppressed or exploited by the practices and operation of organizations of another more dominant racial group. It is group rather than individual behavior. Racist practices and conditions have been going on for so long that they often seem natural; individuals are often unaware that they are perpetuating an unfair system.

Intercultural marriage (see *interracial marriage* and *interfaith marriage*)— This refers to marriage between members of different cultural groups.

Interfaith marriage (see *intercultural marriage*)—This term is used increasingly to refer to marriage between individuals from two of the broader divisions of religion such as Christianity, Judaism, or Muhammadanism. It is not synonymous with interreligious marriage, but the two terms are often used interchangeably.

Intermarriage (see *interfaith marriage, intercultural marriage,* and *interracial marriage*)—This broad term denotes marriage across religious, racial, ethnic, or other social divisions. Often it is used wrongly to mean interracial marriages only.

Interracial marriage (see *intercultural marriage*)— This defines marriage across racial lines. The term also is used to refer generally to interethnic marriages.

Interreligious marriage—This is marriage between members of different denominations and/or sects, usually when both are within the Christian faith.

Marriage—Marriage is a legal, usually religious, rite that establishes a family as a social, nurturing, economic, and, potentially, child-bearing unit. Marriage joins two people and two networks of relatives and/or friends.

Perhaps it would be helpful here to take a closer look at marriage in order to stimulate thinking about the serious, complex relationships it represents. Stahmann and Hiebert (1980, 25-39) see marriage as multidimensional, or as a relationship that functions on many levels. It has a social dimension which includes companionship and special sharing in interpersonal activities. Its geographical dimension means shared space and physical nearness. The sexual dimension means a unique kind of sharing of the physical, sensual, sexual, and reproductive aspects of two people. In the emotional dimension, partners share emotional and phantasy levels of life.

The intellectual dimension includes thought processes, planning, and shared thinking about life and goals. The economic dimension covers sharing the accumulation, use, and distribution of money. The recreational dimension embraces the sharing of activities that replenish and renew and keep a relationship alive. The religious dimension includes sharing values and attitudes about living and the meaning of life. The legal dimension means participation in the incorporation of a relationship in the civil and legal processes of society. The glue that binds all of the dimensions together is the bonding process that develops into commitment.

However, viewed cross-culturally, marriage takes on some added dimensions. It is frequently a relationship between groups rather than just a relationship between two individuals. It is not only a sexual relationship; it may be a form of exchange involving the transfer of rights and obligations between the contracting parties. All societies have restrictions, taboos, and exogamous and endogamous boundaries. Comparatively few societies limit their members to one spouse (Augsburger 1986, 178).

Minority—A minority is a group that has lesser status and power (not necessarily fewer members). It is usually discriminated against and subjected to differential or unequal treatment.

Miscegenation—This refers to the interbreeding of what are presumed to be distinct human races, especially marriages between white and non-white persons.

Mixed marriage—A mixed marriage is between members of different religious, racial, ethnic, or national groups.

Prejudice—Prejudice is an attitude or state of mind characterized by negative concepts, feelings, and action orientations regarding the members of a particular group. One can be prejudiced toward a person as an individual, toward a group, or toward a person as a member of a group. Prejudice usually leads to discrimination.

Races—Races are populations that differ in the incidence of certain genes or inherited traits but together are capable of producing mixed children (Vander Zanden 1979, 624). Races may differ in skin color, hair texture, facial features, stature, and head shape. They do not differ in intelligence and hereditary abilities.

Stereotype—A stereotype is an unscientific and, hence, unreliable generalization that people make about other people as persons or as groups. It can be an exaggerated idea, image, or belief associated with some category of people. The fallacy of stereotyping is the assumption that the alleged attributes of the category apply to all of its members. This assumption does not allow for individual differences.

The Bottom Line

Why does interracial marriage excite, scare, and anger so many people? Porterfield (1978, 1) decided that "cross-racial sex is one of the most virulent and latently emotional foundations which supports the United States castelike [discriminatory] system." This fear of sexual intermingling is the bottom line, but, of course, there are many lesser layers of fear and prejudice, and even some well-founded concerns regarding interreligious and transracial marriages—especially black-white unions. There is also widespread ignorance and many misconceptions concerning Catholic and Protestant church positions on interreligious marriage. Bolman warned everyone who touches mixed marriages to watch his or her "culturalistic pseudo-insights" (1968).

Those planning intermarriage and those who counsel them must realize that, from mate-choice to (God forbid) the dissolution of a marriage, more factors are operating and greater complexity occurs than in homogamous marriages. No marriage is simple, and any marriage will be complicated by racial and/or cultural differences. Spouses in mixed marriages (and those who might advise or support them) must contend with their own subtle, sometimes unconscious negative attitudes and actions pertaining to the residue of their beliefs about their partners' racial/cultural groups (Baptiste 1984, 374). Cultural differences can mask a personality problem, and vice versa.

Since several recent studies on intermarriage do show that difficulties are more likely to occur in intermarriages than in marriages within one race, ethnicity, or faith, it behooves the friend, supporter, or counselor of the mixed couple to become as well prepared as possible to guide the couple planning such a marriage (Ho 1984, 112). However, studies also show that mixed couples have a tendency to blame any shortcomings in their marriages on religious, ethnic, or cultural factors, and fall back on stereotypes in criticizing each other.

II

CULTURAL GROUPS IN THE UNITED STATES AND HOW THEY RELATE TO EACH OTHER

T his chapter looks briefly at the powerful impact of culture, in general, and at a few significant characteristics of some specific cultural groups. It also discusses some ways two different cultures can interface with each other. The purposes of the chapter are to help counselors relate to their cross-cultural counselees and to guide counselors in dealing with the diverse cultures in a mixed marriage. The chapter posits that an ultimate goal for cross-cultural counselors and counselees is a productive, rewarding relationship between persons who do not initially share the same perceptions, values, orientations, and customs.

Some Thoughts About Applying Intercultural Information

Triandis et al. (1982, 419) express a caution in comparing cultures: a cultural group that sees itself as very high in some trait can tend to see other groups as low in the same trait. Therefore, in evaluating and assessing the impact of a cultural trait of a group other than one's own, the evaluator must be aware of his or her own very natural ethnocentrism.

Culture generally refers to the modal practices within a group—the average or normal expression of language, beliefs, customs, rituals, and ceremonies. But it is a well-known fact that individual members of a cultural group differ substantially in the extent to which they reflect the modal patterns of the group. Individual differences within a group exist because the effects of culture upon individuals are mediated by biologically based temperament, the degree of socialization, the social class, and the type of family structure (Das and Littrel 1989, 9). In fact,

> . . . it is often considered the mark of the sophisticated clinician that he considers all of his clients in terms of the culture groups to which they belong. Yet, in the final analysis, a client who is to be genuinely understood should never be confined to the stereotype of his culture. (Kelly in Ivey 1987, 170)

Acculturation

Since any non-dominant-culture member is in some stage of acculturation, it is helpful to discuss that concept briefly here. Acculturation refers to the process by which those new to a society (or not perceived as a central part of that society) adopt the attitudes, values, and behaviors of the dominant, host culture. It is inappropriate and unwise, therefore, to treat a racial culture or ethnic subculture as a monolithic group (in which all of the members have identical cultures) with a fixed set of behavioral differences. Acculturation may modify the effects even of strong cultural norms (O'Guinn et al. 1987, 79). One indication of acculturation in a bilingual environment is the adoption of the dominant society's language. The ability and the preference to read in that language may be strongly indicative of acculturation.

There are significant differences in the way ethnic and racial groups use language, attach meaning to words, and prefer communication styles. Although the implications for cross-cultural miscommunication are obvious, the ability to speak English is so widespread in the United States that language may not be an important indicator of acculturation.

Culture and Marriage

Rohrlich (1988, 42) emphasizes the importance of facing cultural differences in marriage:

1. To marry an individual from another culture is to marry

that culture as well. Lack of communicated interest or a partner's assumption that a spouse is unattached to his[/her] culture gives rise to the gravest kind of problems. Because behavior is a product of culture, the precepts of that culture must be raised, discussed and valued (if not shared) by both parties.

2. An *awareness* of cultural differences must come before sensitivity and appreciation can be developed. The cultural difference is what makes the fabric of the marriage more varied, interesting, and richer (Rogers, 1977). Cultural differences can be the basis for many constructive dyadic interactions that help both partners clarify expectations as well as verbalize feelings.

Courting couples can easily blind themselves to potentially problematic cultural differences. They tend to minimize the impact of the differences since those in courtship prefer to "accentuate the positive."

Culture and Family

The family represents a critical environment for the development, expression, and maintenance of culturally bound values and behaviors. The structure of the family may significantly influence the relative power, responsibilities, and expectations of its members. Since the family structure is significantly influenced by cultural forces, and this structure helps determine family roles and responsibilities, the importance of understanding this area of two interfacing cultures is obvious (O'Guinn et al. 1987, 79).

Eye Contact Across Cultures

The meaning attached to this non-verbal behavior differs markedly across cultures. Anglo-Americans rely on eye contact; blacks tend to hold steady eye contact when speaking but have less contact when listening. Among some orientals, avoidance of eye contact may mean respect.

Self-Disclosure

Another important area where cultural differences play a vital role is the operation of self-disclosure in marriage. Self-disclosure can be defined as the process of making the self known to others and allowing oneself to be perceived by others. There is a great amount of cultural variation in how one discloses and how much should be disclosed. Where expectations and role perceptions are immediately different (as is likely to be the case when partners are from two different cultures), awareness and discussion of how partners see and disclose themselves permits one spouse to compare his or her impression with the perceived self-image of the other spouse (Rohrlich 1988, 40).

Leigh's warning in Dillard (1983, 151) is good advice with which to end this part of the chapter: "The practitioner sensitive to ethnic concerns must work a fine line between using cultural knowledge for greater understanding or using it in stereotypical ways that block the individualizing of a particular client in a particular environment."

Some Specific Cultural Information

A counselor working cross-culturally or helping others to relate cross-culturally needs specific knowledge of the cultural systems he or she is dealing with. The comprehensive information needed for each specific situation is beyond the scope of this book, but this section indicates some of the categories of needed information and discusses some values, customs, and behaviors of a few of the more prominent cultural systems in the United States.

The following outline of categories of potentially helpful information might serve as a guide to the counselor-student of cultures:

1. Legal and social definitions of the cultural (usually minority) group

2. Socio-economic and political status
3. Health, education, and social status
4. Religious affiliation and values
5. Family structure, relationships, lifestyles, and values
6. Language patterns and use
7. Perceptions of help seeking
8. Historical experiences and patterns of discrimination and/or exclusion (Dillard 1983, 151).

It is important to note that this list includes information concerning the community and the socio-political environment. This emphasizes the fact that individuals, couples, and families do not exist in a vacuum; and to understand them fully, one must know something about the wider social systems of which they are a part.

I'm going to do something dangerous—cite some general cultural characteristics of specific ethnic groups. This is dangerous because it is so easy to decide that a member of a certain group likes or does certain things because "that is what they all do." The knowledge of a specific cultural background can be helpful, but each individual situation must be checked for the impact of individual preferences, family values, and environmental conditioning.

Asian Americans

Although all Asian-Americans are often perceived as sharing the same or similar cultural characteristics, it must be remembered that they are comprised of many diverse groups (Chinese, Japanese, Korean, Filipino, Guamians, Malay Samoans, and Indo-Chinese refugees). Each group has its own language and cultural history. Of course, very large differences exist within each Asian-American group in terms of acculturation, primary language, generational status (immigrant versus fourth or fifth-generation Asian-Americans), and socio-economic status.

Asian-Americans tend to be characterized by an action orientation, a different time perspective (less rigid, with more slow-paced, social-business meetings), an emphasis on immediate, short-range goals, and a concrete, tangible, structured approach. They tend to mask their feelings and to participate in one-way, authority-figure-to-person communication. Silence can show respect for the other person present. Advice-seeking and physical and mental well-being are defined differently than in Western society.

Asian-Americans tend to feel a great deal of stigma and shame in talking about personal problems; emotional problems are private. Some of the values that seem to be common to all of the ethnicities above are the fear of bringing shame to the family, submergence of individuality, somatization of symptoms (making mental symptoms physical), self-control to resolve problems, restraint of strong feelings, and respect for authority.

It is helpful to know the broader values on which certain culture traits or customs are based. For instance, a Filipino wife's relationship to her husband needs to be viewed within culturally accepted roles for women, just as a Japanese son's devotion to his grandparents must be viewed within the concept of filial duty and respect.

In Japanese culture, the emphasis is on group harmony and cohesion. The Japanese tend to be subtle and discreet in handling relationship issues and problems.

Chinese families in the United States are now primarily nuclear. Individuals have more freedom and independence than they did in China, but tend to experience more emotional strains and frustrations. The five classic Chinese virtues (love of all human beings, filial obedience, reciprocity and concern for the welfare of others, attention to ritual and ceremony, and harmony of life with nature) still exert on individuals a pull that is divergent from some mainstream societal values (Augsburger 1986, 166). The Chinese emphasize self-control and internal restraint in their families. They use shame and guilt to discourage individualism. Traditional Chinese-Americans are predominantly Buddhists and Taoists.

American Blacks

American blacks tend to have strong kinship bonds, adaptable family roles, high achievement, strong work incentives, and strong religious ties (Dillard 1983, 139). They tend to be action-oriented, to utilize a less rigorous time perspective (strict punctuality may conflict with other values), and immediate, short-range goals are a significant focus. They often have been affected by the residual results of racial oppression. These can include less openness, suspicion, and verbal game-playing that makes a member of another ethnic group an "outsider." The counselor must remember that non-verbal behavior is an important part of communication (i.e., gestures, use of eyes, and types of laughter). These communications can indicate disdain, uneasiness, anger, and distance.

Blacks in the United States from the West Indies have a multicultural background which includes Amerindian, European, Asian, and African roots. They are ambitious, sedate, self-assured, self-confident, and assertive. They find it difficult to share personal problems with professionals.

Some blacks from Haiti may pretend to be French-speaking when they are not, because of the prestige attached to knowledge of French and the assumption by many Americans that all Haitians speak French (Giles 1990, 318). Of course, French is their first language, and most Haitian blacks speak French.

Nigerians in the United States who are not yet fully acculturated embrace an adult-family, extended-family, and group-oriented culture. Children are reared according to prescribed sex roles and are taught to conceal stress as a matter of pride and endurance. Adults more readily disclose information about their achievements than they do about their feelings. Women fear that their disclosure might embarrass their spouses or their families.

Nigerians might answer "yes" to numerous questions. However, this might be just a polite acknowledgment to an authority figure. The general speech pattern is monotone. Looking directly into the eyes of a speaker may show disrespect, especially if the other person is older.

Mexican-Americans, Puerto Ricans, and Cubans

Hispanics form a broad, Spanish-related cultural group which includes all of the above. Mexican-Americans, Puerto Ricans, and Cubans tend to share an action-orientation, a casual time perspective, a focus on immediate, short-range goals, and a concrete, tangible, structured approach to life. They stress the importance of responsibility to one's family. Authorities on Hispanics stress the importance of machismo (aggressive behavior and chauvinism), but some feel that the significance of this is overstated. Compadres (godparents) and other fictive kin are part of the social structure. Hispanic families tend to have more traditional male-female relationships and are less materialistic than Anglos (Abney-Guardano 1983, 49). The emphasis of Hispanic religious values (and traditional family values) on virginity can impact negatively the status of women. They may be protected from environments where achievement is earned and learned, and the value of beauty and physical attributes is stressed over academic and career recognition. They, therefore, may not be valued for their abilities and accomplishments. Even Hispanic women fluent in English may hold Spanish as the language of emotions.

Although people of Spanish background have been treated here as one large group, it must be remembered that those in the United States are really divided into several groups with marked differences according to their countries of origin. One must also keep in mind the acculturation process when studying these cultures.

Although Mexican-American families appear more patriarchal relative to Anglo or dominant society norms, they are dynamic units whose roles are in the process of changing toward a more egalitarian family structure (O'Guinn et al. 1987, 80).

The degree of acculturation of Mexican-Americans is very important when counseling them. The *Acculturation Rating Scale for Mexican-Americans* (Cuellar et al. 1980) positions counselees on a five-category continuum: (1) very Mexican; (2) Mexican-oriented bicultural; (3) "true" bicultural; (4) Anglo-oriented bicultural; and (5) very anglicized.

Mexican-Americans identify strongly with family, community, and ethnic group; they tend to personalize interpersonal relationships; their family problems may have a higher priority than individual needs; and they are primarily Catholic.

Puerto Ricans are United States citizens on their home island or in the United States. They are a mixture of Taino Indian, African, and Spanish, and they come in all colors. In addition to the values discussed above, Hispanics stress an inner sense of dignity and the respect of that dignity by others. Since many Puerto Ricans move back and forth between the island and the mainland, their level of acculturation must be assessed accordingly.

Close ties exist between family and extended family members. Distantly related and even non-related children are often treated as family. Although often bilingual, Puerto Ricans tend to converse more freely in Spanish.

Native Americans

Native Americans (American Indians) likewise tend to be action-oriented, to have a different time perspective, to value immediate short-range goals, and to have concrete, tangible, structured speech. They are family oriented and stress group-centered cooperation. They also stress giving over saving, and respect for age rather than emphasis on youth. They have important religious mind-body distinctions (mental illnesses can have physical symptoms and physical illnesses can have mental symptoms) and a less direct pattern of communication. The individual must be considered within the context of the community.

Some other characteristics that seem to be common to the hundreds of tribes in the United States are tribal loyalty, reticence, humility, and an avoidance of personal glory and gain. Religion, though often varied and non-Christian, functions as a strong spiritual force among most Native Americans. Parents are permissive and emphasize children's freedom, responsibility, and autonomy. Possessions and duties are shared within and among families. There are many languages and dialects among tribes, but most native-Americans are bilingual. They tend to appear passive and to be non-intrusive, even in a counseling situation.

LaFramboise et al. (1990, 638) list five levels of acculturation for Native Americans:

1. *Traditional*—These individuals generally speak and think in their native language and know little English. They observe "old time" traditions and values.
2. *Transitional*—These individuals generally speak both English and the Native language in the home. They question basic traditionalism and religion, yet cannot fully accept dominant culture and values.
3. *Marginal*—These people may be defensively Indian, but are unable either to live the cultural heritage of their tribal group or to identify with the dominant society. This group tends to have the most difficulty in coping with social problems due to their ethnicity.
4. *Assimilated*—Within this group are the people who, for the most part, have been accepted by the dominant society. They generally have embraced dominant culture and values.
5. *Bicultural*— . . . Within this group are those who are, for the most part, accepted by the dominant society. Yet they also know and accept their tribal traditions and culture.

The counselor should note that social class standing can affect all of the above behaviors and values. Middle-class membership moves all of the minorities and the majority groups closer together.

The cross-cultural counselor must: (1) resist ethnocentric biases, (2) be sensitive to societal pressures against intermarriage, and (3) be accepting of intra-familial cultural differences (Baptiste 1984, 379).

The counselor should be able to position cross-cultural counselees within three levels:

1. *Individual Level.* This level recognizes that all of us are unique in some respects, regardless of whether we are from the same race, culture, gender, ethnic group, or family.

2. *Group Level.* This level considers race, culture, ethnicity, gender, and religious affiliations. These are more difficult to deal with because of the emotional connotations and stereotypes tied to groups.

3. *Universal Level.* We are all human beings, and, as such, we share similarities that cut across whatever racial/ethnic identity group with which we are involved (Ivey et al. 1981, 14-15).

In cross-cultural counseling, one tends to interact on the individual and universal levels.

The following list shows human universals that were drawn from over 300 cultural groups (Murdock in Augsburger 1986, 51):

Human Universals

Age grading	Decorative art	Fire making
Athletic sports	Divination	Folklore
Bodily adornment	Division of labor	Food taboos
Calendar	Dream interpretation	Funeral rites
Cleanliness training	Education	Games
Community organization	Eschatology	Gestures
	Ethics	Gift giving
Cooking	Ethnobotany	Government
Cooperative labor	Etiquette	Hair styles
Cosmology	Faith healing	Hospitality
Courtship	Family	Housing
Dancing	Feasting	Hygiene

Incest taboos	natural functions	Puberty customs
Inheritance rules	Mourning	Religious ritual
Joking	Music	Residence rules ·
Kin groups	Mythology	Sexual restrictions
Kinship nomenclature	Numerals	Soul concerns
Language	Obstetrics	Status differentiation
Law	Penal sanctions	Surgery
Luck superstition	Population policy	Toolmaking
Magic	Postnatal care	Trade
Marriage	Pregnancy usages	Visiting
Mealtime	Property rights	Weaning
Medicine	Propitiation of supernatural beings	Weather control
Modesty concerning		

Summary

This chapter includes basic cultural information on some significant racial and ethnic groups in the United States. It considers the use of such information by a dominant society counselor in cross-cultural counseling. The group-specific cultural material covered must be applied sensitively and in consideration of a number of mitigating factors.

III

CHARACTERISTICS AND
DYNAMICS OF
MIXED MARRIAGES

The possibility of a mixed marriage (especially involving someone close) tends to evoke many fears and strong feelings in relatives, friends, and even strangers. This chapter reviews some of the literature and discusses some of the beliefs concerning interracial marriage. Some are supported by research and some are not. It includes some myths based on prejudice and some cautions based on fact.

Here is one truth that has a scientific basis: "There is no evidence of innate racial distinctions that could be relevant to marriage except those which have been created historically institutionally" (McDowell in Porterfield 1978, 13). In other words, the significant factors which cause concern regarding interracial marriages and whatever is related to intermarriages that causes them to succeed or fail are taught or developed by society. Genetically, any member of homo sapiens (the human race) is equipped to relate to, and to intermarry with, any other member of the species from anywhere in the world. The differences that adversely affect relatability are learned and taught. Of course, such learning may become deeply ingrained in the personality structures of individuals in a given society.

Society Has Something to Say About
Interracial Marriage

The main attitudes of the majority of the people in a society become a collective pressure which shapes how people feel and what they do. Society speaks through implied and usually unwritten cultural pressures that affect everyone's decisions as "shoulds" or "should nots." Those who study mate choice have developed some theories to explain how society controls interracial marriage. These theories are expressed as patterns that potential marriage partners follow as they choose each other under the influence of each partner's membership group and the broader society's expectations. About the only idea that all of the experts agree on is that homogamy tends to be a consistent factor in mate choice. Age, educational level, and occupational level of both partners tend to be similar in a transracial marriage as well as in same-race marriages.

Other ideas explaining the selection of partners in racially mixed marriages are not as widely supported. Jansen (1982, 225) explains that when several ethnic groups meet each other repeatedly over time, three possible outcomes can affect intermarriage: (1) One group (or more than one) can be assimilated into another group (or other groups). The chief process in assimilation is acculturation—one culture displacing the others. (2) The "melting pot" theory can become operative. The chief process here is intermarriage. (3) Cultural pluralism can become the most significant way that two different ethnic or racial groups relate. The relationship between the groups will be harmonious but intermarriage will also take place. Those concerned with "racial purity" see none of these three outcomes as desirable. Although intermarriage is listed as a part of the "melting pot" and the cultural assimilation possibilities, it comprises such a small percentage of all marriages that it is usually an isolated happening that is not surrounded with a friendly, "melted" atmosphere in the United States.

Murguia (1986, 96) uses the exchange theory of mate selection to explain choices in Hispanic-white marriages. A Spanish-surnamed female can gain (1) white physical features in her children; (2) a white surname; (3) an increase in social class standing, and (4) greater equality in the marriage relationship.

The Anglo (white) male gains a husband-and-family-oriented spouse. Of course, an exchange of desirable characteristics and resources can be a way of explaining many within-group mate choices.

At the stage in life when people are choosing life partners, a lot of other developmental things should be taking place in their lives. Schlossberg (1984, 21) includes Erikson's developmental stages to delineate what these other important developments should be. The completion of individual identity development should take place in the early twenties. However, sexual identity becomes more complicated when "lines" are crossed, since masculine and feminine traits are somewhat culturally determined. Part of the basis for the resolution of individuality is a feeling of continuity between the past and the present; such a feeling is difficult to maintain when an interracial marriage causes a significant change in social networks, relationships with parents, etc.

The development of intimacy should cover ties with a spouse, with parents, with other relatives, and with friends. Intimacy is marked by free interchange and disclosure, by reciprocal expressions of affection, and by mutual trust, empathy, and understanding. Interracial marriage has the potential of limiting communication among all of the relationships above except, perhaps, the marital pair. Women usually do much better than men in establishing intimacy, but some research shows that white men and women tend to have difficulty separating from their parents and establishing new relationships (Kelley 1976). Other studies have shown that most white families, especially the parents, initially become alienated from their child who marries a black (Benson in Gibbs 1987, 266).

Most of the white mixed-marriage partners I interviewed in preparation for this book experienced temporary rejection by their parents. When Joan Mitchell's parents first learned that she was dating and thinking of marrying a black man, they were very upset and forbade her to see him. After much discussion and argument, Joan moved away to live with Sam. About two years after her marriage, which only her brother attended, her parents remained distant and estranged. Finally they agreed to let Sam visit them. They were quite impressed with him and began to warm up to him. They finally accepted Sam fully and adored their grandchildren. They visited and telephoned back and forth as if there were no racial differences.

When Rose Dombrowski's father learned that she was secretly dating Dan, a black fellow, he became verbally vicious. When she moved in with Dan, her father sent her a letter disowning her. She and Dan went ahead with their marriage; when their first child was born, her father came to visit them. Time and the gradual realization that Dan is a responsible person have brought about a close relationship between Rose and Dan and her parents. The parents now enjoy the grandchildren and share holidays.

Ron Wilson (white) felt that his parents were generally accepting of his marriage to a black woman even when they first heard about it. Their major objection was the religious difference.

The motivation for a mixed marriage comes from a combination of conscious and unconscious factors in interaction. For this reason, and because the engaged partners are so intensely involved, it is unrealistic to expect them to be completely objective about their motives. Matters can become further complicated if they resent the advice of others and, in reaction, they move toward an unwise decision regarding marriage.

Motives for a mixed marriage can be the same as for same-race unions. People can "run into each other" or be "thrown together," especially in circumstances in which there are few members of the opposite sex and few from the seeker's own racial or ethnic group. Marriage as a means of gaining financial security or social status is not unusual in within-group marriage or intermarriage. A more questionable motive for intermarriage is the fulfillment of a need based on a stereotype such as "the women (or men) of that other group are more sexy." The predominant cause attributed to mate choice, in general, should be viewed increasingly as the dominant cause in less-common forms of wedlock such as interracial marriage.

The idea that mate selection is accidental or by chance is not supported by the literature on the subject (Stahmann & Hiebert 1980, 16). People do make decisions based on what they think they need at that time. However, their perceptions may be faulty and their need may not be realistic. As homogamy based on traditional categories (race, religion, and social class) slowly declines, homogamy based on personal characteristics can be expected to become increasingly the primary factor in mate selection (Porterfield 1978, 69).

Attitudes Do (Slowly) Change

Many of the people who have agreed that public facilities should be desegregated, and that there should be equal opportunity for jobs, remain skeptical and even hostile regarding racial intermarriage (Turner 1982, 61). A 1978 Gallup Poll showed that 60% of the United States populace disapproved of marriage between blacks and whites. It is still a fact in this country that the color of a person's skin can have more to do with one's life chances than the quality of one's mind or the diligence of one's efforts.

In 1971, a Harris Poll was summarized thus in *Life* magazine: "Fear of interracial marriage expressed by the white population is based in part on traditional attitudes, in part on social pride, and in part on the fear of losing social-caste status" (Harris 1971, 66). One of the notions on which this negativism is based is the "inherent inferiority" of black people that is bolstered by religious pronouncements on the curse of Canaan in the Bible. This biblical interpretation, discussed in a later chapter, is no longer accepted by most Bible scholars. Another facet of the negative picture is the tendency of whites who are basically on a lower level of social status to have greater opposition to intermarriage than their middle- and upper-class counterparts. Another support for negative white attitudes is the realization that black people have been assigned to an inferior position in this society; this realization then becomes a rationalization for feelings against racial intermarriage.

At one time or another in our history, 40 of the 50 states had laws against black-white intermarriage. Some also prohibited marriage between whites and West Indians, Japanese, Chinese, Mongolians, Indians, and Malayans (Cretzer and Leon 1982, 3). Of course, all of these laws were declared unconstitutional in 1967. Both before and after that Supreme Court decision, different groups in society had their own usually unwritten but quite explicit rules about who may marry whom. Constraints on intermarriage are based on religious, political, cultural, social class, and/or racial/ethnic differences. Pressure to marry within one's race is always strong.

The prevalent code of sex morality in American society includes race prerogatives and sex prerogatives. This means that males have greater freedom to initiate dating or sex overtures. Since whites also traditionally have prerogatives, white males have greater freedom to initiate sex overtures with black females without as much pressure eventually to marry them (Porterfield 1978, 87). Black males have sexual but not race prerogatives. These attitudes have become more positive since 1978, but interracial dating is still a matter of some controversy. Children of mixed marriages may encounter especially painful difficulties socializing as teenagers (see chapter 5). In our relatively segregated society, young people have not been in contact with other ethnic groups at the dating period. But such contacts have been increasing. Therefore, we can expect the rate of interracial marriage to increase. In the last 20 years, it has increased and this trend is accelerating.

In areas of life in which intimate relationships are fostered and involved, whites show a decided desire for segregation while blacks are much less interested in this form of racial separation.

However, since the emergence of Black Pride, more blacks have come to view interracial marriage as undesirable.

One of the devices that helped keep the racial caste system functioning in the United States was the societal custom of defining all persons with any black ancestry as black. Thus, a single black ancestor—one in eight or one in sixteen—was presumed sufficient to make an individual unacceptable as a member of the dominant white caste (Porterfield 1978, 3). Most blacks and whites still consider any black blood as categorizing that individual as black. What is notable is that this system does not stay valid for all of the racial mixtures in America. A white person with a native American as one of eight great-grandparents is not considered Indian but white and can boast about that ancestor's connection with a warrior nation such as the Cherokees, the Comanches, the Apaches, or the Sioux.

Gurak and Fitzpatrick (1982, 921-922) predict that there will not be a large number of transracial marriages in the United States until some form of social proximity of large numbers of people from different ethnic backgrounds will have evolved into a common aspect of life. Heterogeneity in national origin, mother tongue, birth region, education, and occupation raises the rate of intermarriage. Of course, the opportunities for persons from diverse backgrounds to meet and mix steadily increases.

Following is a summary of the social forces which tend to prevent mixed marriages: (1) the segregated social structure of our culture; (2) the system of attitudes, beliefs, and myths which grows out of the social system and which serves to strengthen it; (3) the laws which express the sex and marriage customs of the culture (usually no longer a part of the legal system); (4) institutional functionaries such as clergy, army officers, and government employees who attempt to discourage interracial marriage (since it is not legal, this effort is no longer obvious or direct); and (5) the family, especially the immediate family, which uses affectional ties and the withdrawal of material support to prevent intermarriage.

What Kind of People Intermarry?

Kelley (1976) did an in-depth study of ten black and white married couples in England. He found that significant factors in his subjects' mate choices included similarity in age, educational level, and occupational level. In fact, they had choice motivations similar to non-mixed couples except for non-conformist belief patterns, lower levels of racial prejudice, and lower levels of ethnic identity. The partners tended to share residential proximity, ethnicity, religion, and social class. The similarity and complementarily between the partners' personalities indicated that the normal, usual factors in mate choice were operative. Although England is not the United States, that society is similar enough to ours to provide some informative suggestions on mate-choice motivations.

I conducted in-depth, structured interviews with six individuals in interracial marriages—one black female and her white spouse, one white female and her black spouse, one white female whose black spouse was unavailable, and one black male whose white spouse postponed the interview perpetually. All of the persons interviewed tended to be outgoing and independent. They demonstrated these traits early in life—usually by their teens. They did not depend on conformity or the approval of their peers, and they often made choices against their parents' wishes.

Some more neurotic reasons for mixed marriages could be valid for some marriages but are not substantiated as significant by the mixed-marriage literature. For example, (1) the marriage may be an attempt by one partner to express hostility, exert control, or get revenge; (2) whites may marry blacks to demonstrate their liberalism or idealism; (3) a person may also participate in a mixed marriage because of the lure of the exotic or psychosexual attraction of "otherness"; and (4) the marriage could be a form of rebellion against parents or some other authority. These choices can be made as a repudiation of one's own group; they can express self-hate or self-degradation. *People also may marry interracially simply because they are in love.* (Porterfield 1978, 84).

Interracial couples tend to be older when married than non-mixed couples, and more of them have been previously married. The individuals were often socially isolated from their families before marriage, even before choosing transracial friends. In fact, the family and friends of the white partner frequently did not know of the interracial courtship.

Transracial couples, on the average, have longer courtships than black-black and white-white couples. Joan knew Sam for over a year and lived with him for two years before they married. Ron and Glenda dated and courted about seven years before they married. One interviewee had a two-year courtship, but one married after only a six-month acquaintance.

In Porterfield's study (1978), the interracially married usually lived in black neighborhoods. This was not a consistent choice of residence for the mixed-race couples studied, but the interracial marriage writings stressed the fact that mixed-race couples were often more comfortable in mixed-race or black communities. This was based on the fact that such marriages are more accepted by blacks than by whites, and the couples' friends were mostly black. Porterfield's mixed couples tended to be isolated from other interracial couples, but other studies show that mixed couples tend to list other mixed couples as their close friends.

Cretzer and Leon (1982, 4) note that second-generation immigrants tend to join interracial unions more than first-generation immigrants, and third-generation members intermarry more than the second. They add another factor that increases the possibility of transracial marriage—rural, non-farm residence. The research-supported findings above strongly suggest that the major portion of the current interracial dating and marriage is not related to some pathological abnormality or to any crusade against prejudice. The societal views of interracial marriage expressed above should be viewed dynamically; the picture is ever-changing. Attitudes toward interracial marriage are steadily becoming somewhat more positive in almost every part of the country.

It is regrettable that the literature is limited on the dynamics of interracial marriage in a Christian context. However, I believe that most of the findings discussed here can readily be applied to Christians.

Generalizations, even those supported by research, can never be applied to an individual member of the subject group without taking into consideration much idiosyncratic information. The generalizations should be used as background for a thorough study of a specific situation.

Summary

The literature on interracial marriage cited here discusses some of the characteristics and demographics that tend to be common among those who intermarry. It includes some familial and societal reactions that are sometimes racism-related. The chapter mentions some cautions regarding the application of this knowledge to specific individuals.

IV

INTERDENOMINATIONAL
AND INTERFAITH MARRIAGE

I n seeking direction from counselors or relevant literature such as scripture, one can easily bias her or his findings by operating from a prejudiced position and, consciously or unconsciously, seeking evidence to support that position. In the emotionally charged atmosphere of interracial, interreligious, and interfaith marriage, feelings and fears can easily distort facts. The Bible, written as it was by many different people over several centuries, applies specifically to geographical and historical settings that are now distant. More generally, it provides principles to guide all human relationships in all ages. This chapter represents my understanding of the biblical principles related to mixed marriages. I realize that others may interpret these scriptures differently.

My Interpretation
of Some Bible Texts

"Be ye not unequally yoked—" (2 Corinthians 6:14)
This portion of the verse is interpreted in many different ways by many different people. The incomplete statement easily can be taken out of context. The complete statement, in context, refers to any alliance which might compromise gospel purity; this certainly would include mixed marriages that unite those who serve God with those who do not.

"And hath made of one blood all nations of men for to dwell on all the face of the earth—" (Acts 17:26)
Most Bible readers understand this to mean that all mankind comes from the same stock; the physical characteristics that

distinguish individuals from one another are comparatively minor. In other words, God sees the racial, ethnic, and national barriers that people erect as just that—barriers to be eradicated by the power of the gospel: "There is neither Jew nor Greek, there is neither bond nor free, there is neither male nor female: for ye are all one in Jesus Christ" (Galatians 3:28). In Acts 10:34, Peter explains that God is "no respecter of persons." This means that God does not distinguish between, or accord status to, persons on the basis of outward appearance; He makes no status distinctions concerning social rank, knowledge, wealth, nationality, or race.

> Be ye not unequally yoked together with unbelievers: for what fellowship hath righteousness with unrighteousness? and what communion hath light with darkness? And what concord hath Christ with Belial? or what part hath he that believeth with an infidel? . . . wherefore come out from among them, and be ye separate, saith the Lord, and touch not the unclean thing; and I will receive you. (2 Corinthians 6:14, 15, 17)

This is a loud, clear, and oft-repeated prohibition against interfaith and interreligious marriage that is just as strongly stated in the Old Testament. It is a warning against any and every kind of association with "unbelievers" that would place "believers" in situations where they find it difficult or impossible to avoid *compromising principle.* Of course, this prohibition includes the marriage relationship (see Exodus 34:16; Deuteronomy 7:1-3; Joshua 23:11-12; Ezra 9:1-2).

God's original purpose for Israel, the nation that He set up, was to occupy the land of Canaan, dispossess the inhabitants, and keep strictly separated from them. But any individual "heathen" could become one of God's nation by embracing its belief system. "And if a stranger sojourn with thee in your land, ye shall not vex him. But the stranger that dwelleth with you shall be unto you *as one born among you,* and thou shalt love him as thyself. . . " (Leviticus 19:33-34, italics added). Numbers 15:15 says the same thing even more clearly: "One ordinance shall be both for you of the congregation, and also for the stranger that sojourneth with you, an ordinance forever in your generations: as ye are, so shall the stranger be before the Lord." The more sinful the outside group and the more their religious practices deviated from Israel's established practices and beliefs, the stronger were the prohibitions against mixing. But since members of these proscribed nations could join the Israelite religious system and be regarded as regular members, the problem was with the belief system and not with the nationality or race.

Numbers 12 tells an interesting story of interracial marriage. Moses, under God, was the leader of Israel. The second and third persons in command were his brother and sister, Aaron and Miriam. Moses' wife was a Midianite and, though a descendant of Abraham, she was somewhat darker than most of the Israelites. However, she was a sincere member of the Israelite belief system and her father was a respected orthodox priest. Since the time of Moses' marriage, Miriam had been unhappy about his marrying out of his race. Jealousy arising from a current situation caused Miriam and Aaron to focus on Moses' marriage and to gossip about his Ethiopian wife. The Lord dramatically demonstrated His displeasure with Miriam's envy of Moses and her prejudice against Moses' wife.

Perhaps the most significant scripture used in support of the doctrine of "inferior" and "superior" races (with the implication that members of the two races must not intermarry) is Genesis 9:19-27. When Ham disrespected his drunken father, Noah, his two brothers respected and attempted to restore the father's dignity. Ham's attitude and actions were an indication of his character, and God foresaw that some of his descendants would learn from and copy Ham's negative character traits. God prophesied through Noah: "Cursed be Canaan; a servant of servants shall he be unto his brethren" (Genesis 9:25). Canaan was one of the four sons of Ham (Genesis 10:6). His descendants were the Canaanites—a cruel, warlike group of nations that practiced degrading, licentious idolatry. God's instruction to the Israelites who were to occupy Canaan was to totally eradicate the Canaanites. It was noted above that this was because of their belief system which was opposed to the Israelites' belief system. Canaanite individuals who were willing to change could join the Israelites.

Descendants of Ham's other three sons have at times ruled the world or otherwise occupied very prominent positions. These forebears of the present black or Negroid ethnic groups included Ethiopia, Egypt, and Babylonia (see Genesis 10:6-20). In fact, black nations probably ruled the world during more of the world's history than nations of any other racial group.

In spite of the blessings Noah passed on to his son, Shem, in Genesis 9:26, God allowed his descendants (the Jews) to experience extremes of good and bad fortune, including rulership and servitude, according to the vicissitudes of their allegiance to God or their rejection of Him. There are no greater or more extensive blessings on any earthly people in all of the Bible than those pronounced on the Jews. But God's blessings are conditional, and after the Jews repeatedly failed Him, they became a byword for suffering persecution, pogroms, and near-genocide.

The passage in Genesis 9 has been used by many to support the notion that God has permanently relegated all black people to inferior status, to servitude, and to less natural ability when compared to other races. It would naturally follow, then, that it would be morally wrong for blacks to intermarry with whites or with other races. A number of ministers taught this up until a decade or two ago. Of course, this notion, like most prejudice, dies hard.

According to my understanding of scripture, the Bible does not oppose interracial or international marriage. It does clearly and consistently prohibit interfaith marriage. The same scriptures that provide counsel on interfaith marriages raise questions about interreligious or interdenominational unions because of the differences in belief systems. It is certain that others hold differing views of these scriptures. However, readers and counselors must take into account the strong feelings and rampant prejudices concerning the entire area of mixed marriages.

Interfaith and Interreligious Marriage Today

In the United States, interreligious marriages are between members of different Christian denominations. Interfaith marriages are between a member of a Christian denomination and a member of the Jewish faith or another non-Christian religion. Major marriage problems can arise between members of two religions with widely different beliefs and practices, or between a devout member of one religion and a spouse with no significant belief system or a lifestyle that is opposed to the church-member partner's beliefs. Most religions discourage, and some almost prohibit, marriage outside of the denomination.

The number of interfaith and interdenominational marriages in the United States are definitely increasing. About 40% of Jews and 45% of Catholics currently are intermarrying (Secunda 1988, 82). As the numbers increase, religious groups are having more contact with each other and there is a gradual but slowly increasing acceptance of such unions. However, even in this more tolerant climate, religious intermarriage presents a unique set of problems for the spouses and families involved.

Marrying out of one's religion entails more than simply changing the religious rules or adding another person's religious customs to one's own. It means stepping onto unfamiliar cultural terrain, which can challenge and often threaten parents, grandparents, friends, and clergy—not to mention one's sense of personal history and identity (Secunda 1988, 82).

Some Denominational Positions on Interreligious Marriage

Some information on the official positions of some denominations on religious intermarriage is considered below. Many of these statements were issued some time ago, but I believe that they have not been changed formally, only that current practices and interpretations tend to be less stringent.

The Catholic Church

Perhaps the most problematic interreligious marriages in terms of numbers and severity of conflict are unions between Protestants and Catholics. The position and expectations of the Catholic church are spelled out in much more detail than those of any of the Protestant churches. Some excerpts from the 1983 Code of Canon Law for the Catholic church follow:

"Without the express permission of the competent authority, marriage is forbidden between two baptized persons, one of whom was baptized in the Catholic Church . . . and the other of whom is a member of a church . . . which is not in full communion with the Catholic Church." (801)

"The local ordinary can grant this permission if there is a just and reasonable cause; he is not to grant it unless the following conditions have been fulfilled:

1. the Catholic party declares that he or she is prepared to remove dangers of falling away from the faith and makes a sincere promise to do all in his or her power to have all the children baptized and brought up in the Catholic Church;

2. the other party is to be informed at an appropriate time of these promises which the Catholic party has to make, so that it is clear that the other party is truly aware of the

promise and obligation of the Catholic party;

3. both parties are to be instructed on the essential ends and properties of marriage, which are not to be excluded by either party" (Coriden et al. 1985, 199).

Some Protestant Church Views on Protestant-Catholic Marriage

"Anglican Communion (including Episcopal Church)"

The Anglican Communion (including the Episcopal Church) warns its members "against contracting marriages with Roman Catholics . . . especially as these conditions involve . . . a promise to have their children brought up in a religious system which they cannot themselves accept" (Pike 1954, 91).

Northern Baptists

Baptist pastors are "urged to inform their young people of the menace to their freedom of the imposed authoritarianism of the Roman Catholic Church, not merely in the performance of marriage but also in the dictated rules regarding the raising of offspring of mixed marriages in the Roman Catholic Church" (Ibid 93).

Southern Baptists

Southern Baptists in their 1951 convention resolved:

". . . we, with our Roman friends, give public warning of the dangers to harmonious home life in mixed marriages; . . . we further urge our young people to refuse to enter upon such [prenuptial] agreements and steadfastly to maintain their own religious freedom and guarantee the religious freedom of their children" (Ibid 94).

Disciples of Christ

Disciples of Christ resolved in their 1950 convention:

"Whereas . . . (notably the Roman Catholic church) officially forbids their adherents to enter marriage with non-adherents except on the condition that non-adherents subscribe to certain agreements, particularly that the children of such a union be trained in the faith of the adherent, . . . we urge our young people . . . that in no event they enter into a marriage contract which places them in a position of disadvantage in their family relationship and in the training of their children" (Ibid 95).

Lutheran Church—Missouri Synod

According to a 1953 convention resolution, the Lutheran denomination is clearly against marriage between Lutherans and Roman Catholics. It feels that the theological orientations of the two communions are "diametrically opposed" and therefore commitment to the rearing of a child in an "opposite" belief system is wrong (Ibid 96).

Methodists and Northern and Southern Presbyterians

The Methodists and Northern and Southern Presbyterians also warn their members against marriages with Catholics (Ibid 97, 98).

Within the last three or four decades, the spirit of ecumenism and other factors probably have softened and otherwise modified the positions of all of the above churches toward interfaith marriage. (The three major faiths in the United States are Protestant, Catholic, and Jewish).

Seventh-day Adventists

This denomination holds a strong position against interfaith and interdenominational marriage and against non-churched/S.D.A. marriages. The *Church Manual* officially states that "Differences regarding religion are likely to mar the happiness of a home where partners hold different beliefs and lead to confusion, perplexity and failure in the rearing of children. Differences concerning the worship of God, Sabbath-keeping, recreation, association, and the training of children often lead to discouragement and finally to the complete loss of Christian experience" (1976, 233-234). Religious mixed marriages involving a Seventh-day Adventist usually are not conducted by Seventh-day Adventist pastors or in Seventh-day Adventist churches.

There seems to be a basic principle which undergirds the positions on religious mixed marriage for both Protestants and Catholics. Pike (1954, 87-90) summarizes it thus:

a parent is under obligation to bring into the life of his child the maximum possibilities of religious fulfillment. This means that he is under responsibility to bring up his child in that religious heritage which he (the parent) sincerely believes is nearest to the full truth; the parent is under obligation to bring into the life of the child that view of Christianity which has the best understanding of God, of man, of man's salvation through Jesus Christ, and best provides the means of grace therefor." Any attempt to contract away the above responsibility becomes highly questionable.

Jewish Religion

Generally, Jews are opposed to interfaith marriages, but some branches of Judaism make some accommodation for it. Orthodox and conservative Jews are still quite actively opposed to intermarriage. Reformed Judaism helps educate mixed-faith couples in the Jewish religion, encourages the conversion of the non-Jewish spouse, and helps ease the couple into the Jewish community (Secunda 1988, 88). It should be noted that the strong, age-old traditions of separateness and distinctiveness make some Jewish-Christian marriages as problematic as Catholic-Protestant marriages. The high rate of Jewish intermarriage coupled with a low Jewish birthrate threaten the future of many Jewish communities.

Some Problems Facing Interdenominational and Interfaith Marriages

A major problem in interfaith marriages is making decisions about the religious training of the children. This problem can be a "sleeper"—whatever agreements were made about the religious training of the children before marriage may be accepted outwardly for years, but they can trigger a crisis when it comes time for baptism into the Protestant church or for preparation for first communion in the Catholic church. As a child faces this formal rite in one church, the parent more aligned with the other church can be pricked in his or her long-dormant conscience and innate belief system. At this stage in the family's development, the counsel in Proverbs 22:6 seems to concern many mixed-marriage parents: "Train up a child in the way he should go; and when he is old, he will not depart from it." The sobering thought of the child's lifetime commitment to a certain direction or religion can cause parents to view their pre-marriage promises in a different light.

Another mixed-marriage problem of a religious nature that can become serious is family planning—decisions concerning *planning* children, the number of children, and birth control. Many Catholics have decided that family planning and birth control are private matters and they do not restrict themselves to the Church-approved method of abstinence or rhythm (periodic abstinence). Others feel that the use of birth-control pills or mechanical devices is wrong. Thus, every sexual contact with a

Protestant spouse who has no scruples concerning birth control becomes a potential source of conflict. This certainly does not promote an exciting, mutually satisfying sex life. It is not surprising that Catholic-Protestant marriages tend to have a higher than average rate of unwanted fertility (Bean 1976, 71).

Holidays can be a season of conflict for interfaith couples. Do Jewish-Christian couples have a tree at Christmas time, or a menorah (seven or nine-branched candlestick), or both? Relinquishing or adapting one's religious rituals for the sake of a partner can be painful because it may go against the grain of tradition instilled in each partner since childhood. A crucial factor in the resolution of such differences is the relationships with the marital partners' parents.

Problems in a religious-mixed marriage can be caused by unresolved parent-child conflicts rather than religion. What appears to be a cultural and religious difference can be a smoke screen for a deeper issue. This can be true especially of one who marries someone of another denomination as an act of rebellion against parents.

Most students of interfaith and interdenominational marriage agree that the best outcome results from one partner joining the other partner's church. Therefore, Jewish and Catholic church authorities encourage both parties to become Jewish or Catholic, respectively. This is more easily accomplished, of course, when one partner is not deeply committed to his or her church of origin. However, the person who gives up her or his religion is not immune to feelings of guilt or anger concerning the loss, even years later.

Partners in interfaith and/or interreligious marriages who hold their religious beliefs deeply and firmly tend to have difficulties in their marriages (Pike 1954). Marriage partners with more casual religious experiences tend to have less conflict.

Summary

In spite of formal and informal prohibitions, interreligious marriages (especially those involving Catholics) and interfaith marriages (especially those involving Jews) continue to increase. The couples involved have five choices in dealing with their situations: (1) both join the man's church, (2) both join the woman's church, (3) each stay in his or her own church, (4) both join a third church as a kind of compromise, or (5) both attend no church at all. This last course is usually not a deliberate choice but an unplanned conclusion, temporary or permanent. The counselor's emphasis needs to be placed on helping couples make the choice that will allow them to pursue their religious life together.

V

WHAT ABOUT
THE CHILDREN?

T his is an anguished and often-repeated cry, but it is also a very important question that needs answering. Since the offspring who result from a mixed marriage are not those who decided to set up the union, they can be seen as potential innocent victims of the marriage.

Much has been written about interracial marriages, but little research has been done and little has been written about the children of such marriages. More needs to be known about the dynamics of ethnicity in the offspring of mixed marriages. Such marriages are minimally tolerated in the United States today, but they enjoy greater legal and social approval among many other peoples and nations (Sebring 1985, 4). However, the attitudes in this country seem to be improving, and there is justification for greater optimism for mixed marriages in the future. The stresses on interracial marriage can be severe, and the parents' ability to cope affects the lives of their children. The decision to intermarry does not mean that the couple planning such a marriage has been completely emancipated from the negative racial attitudes of their society.

Some of the questions that mixed-marriage partners might ask themselves are these: Will our children be labeled "mulattoes" or "half-breeds"? Will they be denied social and economic opportunities because of their mixed-racial heritage? Will they suffer from identity and adjustment conflicts that affect their functioning in school, in their own future marriages, and in societal roles in general?

This chapter addresses the above questions and some of the

potential problems children of mixed marriages face. First we consider the statistical picture and discuss in some depth identity-development concerns. Then we discuss institutional racism and living in a bicultural environment. The chapter ends with some suggestions for counseling parents of mixed-race children. Let me emphasize that the potential problems discussed here do not seriously damage all children of mixed marriages any more than the hazards of being raised in a single-parent family dooms those children to inadequate lives. The things discussed here can: (1) generally inform a counselor or advisor, (2) provide background information for a counselee, and (3) provide information for counseling sessions if the need arises. Since much more information is available on black-white marriages than on other racial mixtures in the United States, I discuss these with the hope that the reader will generalize the information and find it helpful in counseling other mixtures.

Statistics on Children of Racially Mixed Marriages in the United States

Gordon (1964, 263) wrote that in 1960, 80% of blacks in the United States were racially mixed. Thus, mixed black-whites can be considered a part of the larger black culture. This chapter concerns the children that result from mixed unions; hence, the focus is on "first generation" interracial children—children with one white and one black or other minority parent.

Statistics indicate that approximately 420,000 interracial married couples lived in the United States in 1985 (McRoy & Freeman 1986, 164). In 1988, Brandell (176) cited census figures reporting over 632,000 interracial marriages in the United States, 125,000 of which were black-white marriages. The number of such marriages greatly increased after the last state miscegenation laws were declared unconstitutional in 1967. "For over two decades these marriages have produced biracial children, many of whom are now adolescents and young adults, located primarily in urban areas in the East, the Midwest, and the West Coast. It has been estimated that there are approximately one million interracial children in the U. S. (Gibbs 1987, 265).

Two Theoretical Positions on the Development of Identity in Biracial Children

Identities are meanings the self acquires through social interaction. They are thought to stem from a feeling of consciousness of kind that begins with commonalities of culture. Identity can become a master status—an identity that overrides others' judgments of the self. The question of ethnic identity is particularly acute and potentially problematic for children of mixed ancestry (Stephan in Root 1992, 51). This raises a major question: Do most mixed-heritage individuals develop stable, single-heritage identities (e.g., Korean), or are they more likely to have multiple-heritage ethnic identities (e.g., Korean-white)?

The jury is still out on the answer to this question. There appear to be two almost polar positions, both supported by the literature: the development of a single-heritage identity and the development of a double-heritage identity.

An Emergent Double-Heritage Identity

Children of black-white, as well as other minority-white marriages, can be viewed as a group of mixed-race young people who resist simple racial classification and who have legitimate claims to both majority and minority social castes (*Newsweek* 1984,120). However, their membership in a minority group is more socially acceptable and usually dominates their lives.

Another concern is that marriage across ethnic boundaries inevitably leads to a loss of identity among minority groups and this, of course, affects the children. This result depends to some extent on the parent membership group or other groups the biracial child identifies with.

Some empirical studies of biracial children indicate that their racial attitudes and self-concepts develop differently from those of either black or white children (Gunthorpe 1978; Payne 1977). The following questions are significant: Are the children of (black-white) biracial parents perceived as biracial, black, or white? How are these nuclear families accepted by their extended families, friends, employers, and the black community?

Many interracial couples teach their children to define their racial identity as "mixed," not as black or white. It is encouraging to note that some studies find that biracial children have equivalent or higher levels of self-esteem when compared to their non-mixed peers (Chang 1974, Jacobs 1978), and that interracial children often are more popular with their white peers than are black children, and with black children than are whites (Benson in Sebring 1985, 6).

> Multiple-heritage ethnic identities are commonly found among mixed-heritage individuals. In addition, the ethnic identity of a mixed-heritage individual depends in part upon the group in question. Whereas a slight majority of mixed-heritage Hispanics did have single-heritage ethnic identities, most respondents from the other samples [part-Japanese Americans in Hawaii and a variety of mixed heritage students in Hawaii] did not. (Root 1992, 62)

Multiracial families, parents and children, are taking active and assertive roles in dismantling accepted social definitions of biracial and interracial families. "White fathers of biracial children are increasingly articulating desires for their children to express non-Black aspects of their identities" (Root 1992, 39).

Root found that problems arose in mixed-race children when there was a partial or complete failure to integrate the racial and ethnic backgrounds of *both* parents into a cohesive identity. In a non-empirical study, 50% of the black-white children answered the question, "How do you think about yourself racially?" as mixed-race. The other 50% were divided equally among black, Afro-American, and "unsure how to respond" (230).

In the above study, the 75% of the respondent adolescents who felt positively about themselves and their biracial ties had learned to negotiate an ethnic identity that incorporates positive aspects of their black and their white racial backgrounds (Root 1992, 237).

Stephan (in Root 1992) summarized the consequences of mixed-heritage status:

> Mixed-heritage individuals do not manifest ill effects from rejection by others, or experience difficulties in establishing identities or in reconciling different cultural norms. In contrast, the data demonstrate that there are benefits of mixed-heritage status, including increased contact with the members of one's heritage groups, enjoyment of the cultures of one's heritage groups, facility in languages spoken by one's heritage groups, and intergroup tolerance. (62)

Of course, these very positive results are dependent on an informed, balanced guidance of bicultural self-concept development and attention to the other interpersonal and environmental factors discussed elsewhere in this chapter and this book.

An Emergent Single-Heritage Identity

A probable majority of the authorities on the subject believe that the soundest identity for a biracial child with one white parent is to be raised as a member of the black race. Poussaint (1984) and Porterfield (1978) have noted that interracial (black-white) children most often seem to identify themselves as black rather than white (Brandell 1988, 177). However, some mixed parents feel uncomfortable with stressing their children's blackness and want them to be proud of both their black and their white heritage. Of course, they can develop primary identity in one race while learning about their other racial stock.

Developmental Factors and Problems of Biracial Identity Development

Two of the factors that facilitate the development of positive racial identities in children of mixed-race parentage are: (1) children are encouraged to acknowledge and discuss their racial heritage with parents and other significant individuals, and (2) parents are able to perceive their child's racial heritage as different from their own and are willing to make changes in their lifestyle conducive to the development of a positive racial identity in the child (McRoy & Freeman 1986, 167).

Some parents deny that race or color is an issue and exhort their children to think of themselves as neither white nor black but human. A second group promotes a black identity in their children and immerse themselves in the black community. Now a growing number of parents attempt to socialize their children to have a dual or biracial identity.

A biracial child may reject one parent as a figure for "identification" and thereby experience massive guilt and disloyal feelings. A girl may find it difficult to identify with a white mother in spite of the mother's constant affirmation of the beauty of the daughter's hair and skin. Ambivalence over racial identity has also been cited as a highly significant problem for biracial children.

If the biracial child is brought up in a nurturing and empathetic parental environment, the child develops into a capable and whole adult. Cauce et al. in Root (1992, 219) did a small-sample study of the social adjustment of biracial youth. None of their results indicate greater difficulties in adjustment than that of non-mixed adolescents. In addition, self and maternal reports show remarkable similarities to the comparison group in peer relations, stress, behavior problems, and self-worth.

Identity Development in the Preschool Years

One of the important developmental experiences of the preschool child, according to Erikson (1963), is the increasing awareness of self and awareness of differences in the people in his or her environment. This can include the differentiation of feelings about self and others who are ethnically different. During this period, the child becomes increasingly aware of racial differences and learns labels and emotional responses associated with various ethnic groups, including his or her own (McRoy & Freeman 1986).

> There are two basic processes involved in the development of racial identity. The first, racial conception, is concerned with when and how the child learns to make racial distinctions at a conceptual level. The second process, racial evaluation, deals with when and how the child evaluates his or her membership in a racial group. In the development of children, the processes by which they learn 'who they are' and 'the value of who they are' are closely related. (Proshansky and Newton in McRoy and Freeman 1986, 165)

Not everyone agrees that children learn this much about racial distinctions this early. Ernest Porterfield (1978) found that the information received from children under six years of age was too fragmented and limited to be of use in an objective determination of their self-concepts. But, on the other hand, Jacobs (1978) was able to identify two distinct stages preschool children go through in the formation of a racial identity. Stage I children had not yet formed definitive concepts of color determination and had no racial sorting system. By about age four children enter Stage II. They can then more consistently recognize color and they internalize racial labels. At some point during this stage, they develop an ambivalence about their own racial status. This can be viewed as a constructive attempt to explore ethnic differences and to achieve a personal framework for the disparities (Sebring 1985, 4).

Gunthorpe (1978), in a study of three- to five-year-old black, white, and mixed-race children, found that interracial children were able to match dolls of varying skin tones with their own skin color. In contrast, black children were inaccurate in these selections and the inaccuracy rate increased with darker skin-toned children. The same research team's review of current studies found little evidence of rejection of own group by blacks or strong ethnocentrism by whites; it did find an increasing tolerance of ethnic differences by all children. Payne's (1977) findings agree with much other research—black children tend to identify with lighter dolls. She also found that interracial children form attitudes regarding racial identification and preference different from their black and white counterparts.

There is general agreement that the issues of early childhood for interracial and black children center around the formation of a healthy self-esteem. A strong sense of self-worth, once established, is unlikely to be severely strained by the issues an interracial child will face later in life. Conversely, a poor self-image can only be exacerbated by later difficulties.

The formation of an ethnic identity can get bound up in parental identification processes. Masculine and feminine stereotypes may be confused with racial ones. For example, if the mother is black and is seen as nurturant, the child may learn to associate nurturing qualities with "blackness" (Sebring 1985, 6).

If the number of studies about this stage is any indication, there seems to be little concern about the identity development of interracial children during latency or the elementary school years. However, the adolescent period shows an explosion of studies on the identity development of mixed-race children.

Identity Development During Adolescence

Erikson (1963) has proposed that the central task of adolescence is to form a stable identity. This includes a sense of uniqueness and self-esteem, the establishment of a sense of autonomy and independence from parents, the ability to relate to same-sex and opposite-sex peers, and the commitment to a vocational choice (263-266).

Several authors have pointed out that identity formation for black adolescents may be more problematic than for whites in view of the devaluation messages the former receive from the dominant society (263-266). Therefore, it would not be difficult to hypothesize that identity formation would be even more difficult for biracial adolescents. In that situation, the normal adolescent experience of rejecting parental figures can be confused with racial considerations. Thus, ambivalence over ethnic identity seems to be the most significant problem faced by interracial adolescents (and younger) children. In a study of 27 racially mixed children in counseling, this conflict was most frequently expressed in attempts to deny their black heritage (Benson 1981). Benson's in-depth study of this group of 3 to 16 year olds revealed that nearly all rejected their black identity verbally, behaviorally, or through social identification with white peers.

Racial identity was the core conflict of the adolescents-in-treatment that Gibbs (1987) described in her study. They described themselves as "half and half," "Heinz' 57 varieties," and "Oreos." For these teenagers, there had been a partial or a complete failure to integrate both racial heritages into a cohesive sense of racial identity. The more frequent tendency was to over identify with the parent who was perceived as the most similar in physical features, especially skin color; the adolescent preferred that parent's racial group and incorporated the perceived attributes of that group. In some cases, the teenager identified with the white parent as a symbol of the dominant majority and rejected the black parent even if there was a closer physical resemblance. Some teenagers were ambivalent and alternately denigrated and praised the attributes of both races.

Some of the teenagers, especially the girls, felt ashamed of their black physical features such as dark skin, curly hair, or broad noses. They rejected black culture as expressed in music and dress styles. They accepted negative attitudes and stereotypes about blacks and tried to distance themselves from blacks. In some cases, the teens over identified with the black parent and rejected white culture and white people. They adopted attitudes, behaviors, and styles of dress of a lower class rather than middle-class black culture, even though most of them were from middle-class, biracial families.

It should be remembered that children in counseling exhibit more problems than children who do not come for counseling. From pre-Civil War days until the Civil Rights movement in the United States, light skin color was associated with economic and personal superiority among blacks. Studies of younger children even now suggest that some vestiges of these sentiments persist among blacks and whites today.

In adolescence, ideas and perceptions are shaped largely by peer standards. According to Logan (1981, 53), black adolescents begin to identify with a sense of "peoplehood" and to question the relevance of using white norms for self-measurement. If a mixed-race adolescent is rejected by peers on the basis of racial background or is unable to discuss racial identity with peers or parents, the transition period can become even more difficult.

In a clinical study of biracial children begun in the late 1960s, Teicher (1968) proposed a series of hypotheses about the sexual identity of this population: (1) Children would identify with the parent seen as less socially depreciated, (2) problems of sexual identity would occur with greater frequency among children whose same-sex parent is markedly different from them in racial characteristics, (3) problems of sexual identity would also occur with greater frequency among children who themselves depreciated the racial characteristics of the same-sex parent or who perceived that the opposite-sex parent depreciates the child's or the spouse's racial characteristics, and (4) the greater the child's problem of racial identification, the greater the problem of sexual identification.

Since possible problems in racial identification and sexual identification are closely related, they raise two important questions for the biracial child: Where do I fit in? and, What is my sexual role? Answering the first question may be complicated for the earliteen. Biracial children who may have had a closely knit peer group and satisfying social relationships in elementary school often experience social problems upon entering junior high or high school. They begin to be excluded from same-sex slumber parties, ski trips, and boy-girl parties. Biracial girls seem to suffer more than boys and report that they are often excluded from high-status social cliques and from sororities. They come to realize that the white boys who are often perceived as the most attractive and desirable usually are not interested in dating them because of the powerful proscriptions against interracial dating in most communities.

"What is my sexual role?" This conflict finds expression in issues of sexual role, sexual identity, choice of sexual partners, and patterns of sexual activity. The gender-identity confusion of biracial adolescents can extend to ambiguities about gender identity or sexual orientation. Females may exhibit very masculine mannerisms in speech, dress, and behavior. Males may become quite effeminate and engage in activities such as shopping with their mothers and gossiping with female friends.

Sexual orientation seems to be more conflictive when the adolescent feels very negative toward the parent of the same sex who is also the minority parent (Tiecher 1968). Choice of sexual partners and patterns of sexual activity are also problematic for biracial teens. Many of them, especially the females, perceive their dating options as limited to other minority adolescents, a group toward which they are often ambivalent and from which they frequently feel alienated. Patterns of sexual activity tend to be an "all or none" situation. Biracial teens who have assumed a militant black identity report higher levels of sexual activity and occasional promiscuity. Alternatively, the teens who have over identified with their white heritage are less likely to be sexually active and more likely to describe sex as being "repulsive or disgusting."

Biracial teens tend to be ambivalent about achievement and upward mobility. Those who have over identified with their version of the black ghetto culture adopt a casual attitude toward school and fear rejection by their black peers if they are perceived as "bookworms." Those who identify with the white, middle-class culture achieve consistency with their peers and aspire for a college education. For biracial teens who come for counseling, the more typical pattern is non-achievement and unrealistic career aspirations.

The stresses faced by racially mixed families are leading growing numbers to seek counseling for the marital dyads and for the children. Studies are inconclusive concerning divorce rates among interracial couples, but some authors suggest the rate is higher than for homogamous couples. Divorces in such families further complicate the lives of biracial children (Sebring 1985, 5). A study of high-risk youth and parents conducted by a San Francisco youth advocacy agency found that 24.9% of the counselees were interracial and that this group reported higher rates of victimization than all other ethnic groups (Gibbs 1987, 267).

Institutional Racism

A major background factor in the social adjustment of children of interracial marriages is the pervasive institutional racism that is a well-documented thread woven through American society. Individual parents of mixed children need to be aware of their personal racism, or reactions to racism, and how this affects their behavior and what they teach their biracial children. The racial identity development of these mixed-race children may be particularly complex because they belong to one racial group that has been positively valued by society and also to another that has been devalued (McRoy & Freeman 1986, 165). Of course, society has historically tended to categorize any person who has any amount of black blood as a member of the black race.

Living in a Bicultural Environment

Opinions differ on the nature and scope of the issues faced by interracial children. There seems to be a strong consensus among many authorities that mixed black children should be considered black. Their position is that the problems faced by these children are the problems of all black children. In a biological sense, interracial children, for all intents and purposes, may be indistinguishable from the larger black culture. A major purpose of some counseling groups formed of white parents of black children is to help the parents raise their children with strong, positive black identities and self-concepts (Hill & Peltzer 1982, 557).

Considerable agreement posits that mixed black children should be raised in mixed or black communities. Their acceptance by the black community seems to be dependent on the children's acceptance of a black identity and their overt expression of some degree of commitment to the mores of the black community (Sebring 1985, 6). In order for the parents of these children to learn and teach the kinds of survival skills which black children need, they should raise their children in black communities, black churches, and around positive black role models. The parents need to know the positive aspects of the black experience and to be able to explain negative black images in an honest, historical perspective.

Mixed-black parents must realize that they are viewed as a part of a minority family—another reason why they need to help their children develop positive black self-images. The child must receive affirmation of him or herself and his/her blackness from the white parent as well as from the rest of the family. McRoy and Zurcher (in McRoy & Freeman 1986, 166-167) found that transracially adopted children develop a sense of belonging and acceptance by identifying with other blacks. A minority opinion is that mixed-race children should not be treated as belonging to one race or the other and should be raised with the concept of mixed identity.

Parents of biracial children need to become aware of their special roles. For example, the white parent needs to know what it means to be a white parent of black children, what his or her feelings are about the children's blackness, and what the local negative societal traits attributed to blacks are. Parents' feelings in these areas are usually conveyed to the children. Some questions that can help bring out these feelings are: What is the racial background of each of the child's parents? How do the parents view the child's racial identity? Does the child have a positive racial self-concept and on what is this judgment based? If a white parent's feelings toward the ethnic heritage of a black spouse are ambivalent or negative, the child's problems will be compounded.

Mixed-race children adopted by white families often have limited contacts with blacks, and their parents tend to de-emphasize their black racial heritage. The parents usually view the children as part-white or mixed, and the children view themselves accordingly. Other transracial adoptive parents take a color-blind attitude and de-emphasize racial identity. Of course, the child follows suit.

Some mothers in a counseling group for white parents of mixed-black children had to struggle with their denial of their children's black identity. A parent in a similar situation identified her child as white, while the teacher and school staff and the child's peers identified him as black. His perceptions were confused and he was unsure of his race, but he wanted to be seen as being like his white peers.

To a lesser extent than parents, siblings and extended-family members can play significant negative or positive roles in the self-concept development of mixed-race children. Grandparents, aunts, uncles, and cousins may not accept such children as relatives or may treat them in an ambivalent, demeaning, or rejecting manner. They also may tease the children or make racist statements about either parent's racial background. If a child is being raised as mixed racially, he or she needs positive role models and peers and supportive kin from both races among the relatives and outside of the family.

Hill and Peltzer (1982, 563) found that white siblings in mixed families frequently were discriminated against by people outside of the family and had to deal with racial incidents related to their black siblings.

The ability to function with two disparate cultures in one's background demonstrates exceptional skills in some mixed families. "Such families exhibit unusual strength, are comfortable with bi-culturality, and exhibit remarkable flexibility, tolerance for ambiguity, comfort with difference, and creativity in their relationships with both the American (dominant society) system and the victim system" (McGoldrick et al. 1982 in Sebring 1985, 7). Of course, "victim system" refers to non-dominant-society minority status in the United States.

Some Implications for Counseling

In counseling transracial families concerning the self-concept development of their children, the usual premise of color blindness must be replaced by an appreciation of the dynamics of the family members' lives as they relate to cultural contexts. Parents need to teach their children individualized "bags of tools" to cope with racism, and practice decision-making skills according to each child's own timing and priorities. In the early stages of counseling the parents, the counselor can be guided by the following questions:

1. What is the racial background of each parent?
2. How do the parents view the children's racial identity? How does each child view his or her own racial identity? Does the child have a positive racial self-concept?
3. What are the child's attitudes and opinions about the two racial groups involved? What are the parents' attitudes?
4. What is the racial make-up of the children's neighborhood and school? What are the racial backgrounds of each child's playmates, schoolmates, and other primary groups? How are the children accepted in these relationships?
5. Does the family provide opportunities for the child to observe positive images of blacks through black magazines, newspapers, church membership, or membership in other black institutions?
6. Do the children have positive black and white role models?
7. How often do the parents and children have social contacts with other blacks or with other whites?
8. How can the parents handle prejudice toward themselves and their children?
9. Are the children experiencing rejection by both blacks and whites?
10. How do the children perceive or feel about self?

Interracial families can be advised to live in communities which are more tolerant of diversity and to network with other interracial families for mutual support. Their ability to discuss and value their children's double heritage seems to be critical for helping the children clarify and develop a positive racial identity. Problems in this area may take a long time to develop and may not be recognized as underlying other more obvious problems. Counselors, therefore, need to improve their knowledge about racial identity issues and become sensitive to their own values and perceptions about mixed-race children.

The counselor also must be sensitive to the racial composition of the community and school and its effect on the development of mixed-race children. Children who are raised in predominantly black or racially balanced schools have a diverse comparison group and often feel more positive about their black racial background than black children raised in predominantly white communities and schools (Williams & Morland 1976 in McRoy & Freeman 1986, 172). Counselors need courses or workshops on racial-identity development and knowledge about community resources such as black archives and literature on black history. One cannot overemphasize that the counselor must guard against his or her personal biases. Such biases can lead to two extremes: an overemphasis of the child's racial background or a denial that the background is at all important.

Counselors—black, white, or mixed—must fully examine their own feelings regarding interracial marriage. They should examine their assumptions about the counselees' cultures. They need to realize that some of the seeming paranoia and scapegoating in black and other minority counselees must be perceived as a viable response to repeated experiences with racism (Sebring 1985, 7).

Parents need help so they can develop in their children the ability to tolerate ambiguity, but the ambiguities should be identified and clarified wherever possible. The children also need to learn how to handle anger.

Jacobs (1978) identified several qualities of parenting that facilitate the formation of a healthy self-concept in interracial children: (1) early ego enhancement (or encouragement and support of individuality and achievement), (2) providing the child with an interracial or racial label, (3) assistance in verbalizing racial material and supportive interest in the expression of racial ambivalence, and (4) multiracial associations. Parents need help in developing the above skills and in assessing how their parenting expectations have been facilitated or negated by the interracial nature of their children. They also need to be prepared for a possible period of rejection by their biracial children.

Parents of teenagers need to help their youngsters distinguish between their own personal interests and abilities and those that have been adopted from a stereotyped notion of their racial identity. They need to see the possible link between their confusion over their racial identity and their confusion over other areas of behavior or developmental tasks. The counselor should guide the parents in encouraging their teenagers to explore both sides of their racial heritage in order to form a positive sense of identification with their ethnic and cultural roots. Teenagers can be assigned "homework" to read so they can report on heroes and write school essays about heroes' achievements representative of both groups. They also can assist in drawing family trees and putting together scrapbooks about their family, friends, and neighbors that illustrate the cultural diversity in their lives.

Teenagers can keep diaries to record their feelings and concerns; they can role play, use creative writing, and fantasize about the future to express their inner feelings. It must be remembered that ethnic or racial identity is a major factor, but it is just one dimension of a number of factors in self-concept.

Chapter 7 offers some suggestions for addressing in counseling sessions questions such as those raised in this chapter.

Summary

Children of mixed-race marriages are at high risk; the formation of their racial identities is complex. However, if the parents are comfortable with who they are, if they choose schools, communities, and friends wisely, and if they accept the reality of their children's racial membership, the risks to the children can be reduced. The most important ingredient in mixed-race children is a healthy self-concept developed from infancy.

Mixed-marriage parents and counselors must be encouraged to become more aware of how they handle their own feelings in order to serve as models in helping the children to deal with their feelings.

VI

CROSS-CULTURAL COUNSELORS' PREPARATION FOR COUNSELING

Know thyself. This age-old admonition is good advice for anyone who counsels in any situation. It is especially so for the cross-cultural counselor whose formal training may not have been counseling. Some form of self-appraisal is a necessity. Trained and untrained counselors both might find it helpful to consider a few areas of awareness that can contribute to effective mixed-marriage counseling.

Each counselor must look within and strive to evaluate his/her own fitness and sensitivity for the counselor role. This includes an awareness of the values and other aspects of a particular culture that are expressed in the counselor's home life, marital adjustment, attitudes, and prejudices. To be blind to this ethnocentrism is to be vulnerable to bias when working with counselees' culture or cultures. Of course, no one can gain a complete and objective understanding of self. But armed with some knowledge and a sense of responsibility, the counselor is, or should be, in a humble and growing state of mind when undertaking the guidance of others toward marriage.

Does the counselor (and the other members of his or her immediate family) have a happy and rewarding family life? Whatever the answer to this question, the counselor needs to understand the impact that personal experience has on what is offered to counselees. For instance, if the counselor's family finances are in chaos after years of marriage, he or she needs to be conscious of what it takes to advise convincingly when "Do as I say" is not "do what I do." If the counselor is not comfortable talking about sex in his or her private life and is unwilling to verbalize the terminology of sex organs, the very important exploration of the congruence of expectations concerning sex is hampered. If the counselor is inhibited and anxious when discussing inner feelings, his or her attitude conveys the message that it is dangerous to attempt that exploration.

The counselor should be careful to separate personal observations and opinions from knowledge gained through careful study and reading. He/she should not substitute the one for the other. If the helper does not have a positive attitude toward the couple planning for marriage, he/she finds it difficult to counsel objectively. And if the helper feels called upon to discourage or condemn the proposed union because of prejudice, the counseling could hardly be considered marriage preparation or be labeled "premarital counseling."

The importance of the counselor's attitude toward intermarriage cannot be overemphasized. In fact, it would be ideal if the counselor is not just neutral but actually believes that an interracial marriage can have the potential of a rich and rewarding relationship. The communication of this hope can encourage the counselees' trust and openness—essential ingredients for successful counseling. Counselees who are not made to feel that they have made a mistake in choosing a partner from another cultural group are more free to express concerns regarding possible problems in the relationship. The role of the counselor is not to encourage or discourage intermarriage; he/she is to assist the counselees in making thoughtful and wise decisions.

One who aspires to the role of counselor and wishes to become useful in helping people make good decisions concerning mixed marriages that will stand the test of time must have a wholesome personality, be well-adjusted to society and to the whole universe, and be emotionally stable, patient, thorough, sincere, and trustworthy. He or she should have a neat and healthy appearance, be tactful and pleasant, and have mature judgment and a genuine interest in people (White 1966). Such a person must be sensitive to cultural differences and should be able to utilize information about different cultures when counseling. Therefore, the culturally skilled counselor is one who has moved from being culturally unaware to being aware and sensitive to his/her own "cultural baggage."

Culturally Biased Assumptions

What is the cultural baggage that everyone learns about from infancy and that can get in the way when one attempts to work across cultures? A major part of it is ethnocentrism—the very natural tendency to look at everything from one's own viewpoint and to be somewhat blind to a sensitive understanding of the other person's viewpoint. The effective counselor also needs a knowledge of the general cultural and social trends which affect both counselor and counselee (such as the community level of subtle prejudice or overt discrimination against the minority group represented). Many otherwise well-educated counselors are surprisingly behind the times when it comes to current knowledge of what is happening in this area. The counselor must be aware of the impact of her/his own family attitudes and family cross-cultural experiences. Some counselors are more knowledgeable of, and empathetic toward, mixed marriages because of personal cross-cultural experiences.

Cross-cultural counselors need to realize that members of the dominant or mainstream society tend to think that everybody thinks as they do and values what they value. Therefore, Western middle-class-oriented individuals (as most counselors are) tend to take for granted the general acceptance of such things as adherence to well-defined time schedules, standard fifty-minute interviews, the importance of promptness, the desirability of long-range goals, openness and intimacy, the importance of verbal communication, and a clear distinction between physical and mental well-being. All of these values are held less firmly but in varying degrees by all other cultural groups (especially those termed "minorities") (Sue & Sue 1990, 34). Thus, most non-WASP (white, Anglo-Saxon, Protestant) groups vary from the above-middle-class norms—they view time as being quite flexible (this includes being on time). Many more intimate things such as sex are not discussed as openly in these groups and are seldom discussed in mixed company. References to mental and physical health symptoms can be blurred, blended, or even exchanged; a person can complain about mental symptoms that are really physical and vice versa.

Related to the above are several assumptions that dominant-society counselors are prone to make.

1. Normal cannot be multimodal. In other words, such things as the average height of men or women or even the average number of meals eaten in a day do not fall into simple numerical patterns when studied across cultures. There may be more than one valid average height or more than one average number of daily meals when considering more than one ethnic or cultural group. The legitimacy of these differences must be taken into consideration when helping members of different cultural groups to blend lifestyles.

2. Individual expression is very important. Actually, some cultural groups prefer group expression. Hence, an individual's lack of competitiveness or lack of drive in creative expression may reflect a need for group support or structures that encourage cooperative activities. Knowing the kind of expression or participation that can reasonably be expected of an individual member of a cultural group helps determine the counselor's approach to counseling and even the structure of the interviews.

3. Someone has to make a change. A bicultural situation requires considerable cross-cultural understanding, especially when making a decision as to when an individual should be encouraged to change or when it would be more feasible to work on changing the social system with which the individual may be in conflict.

4. Independence is preferred to dependency. A value which

may be in operation here may be foreign to the average counselor. This is how dependency on one's relatives and/or peers, as a part of daily lifestyle, is both valued and even essential in some cultures. In the culture of our dominant society, independence for individuals and families is promoted. However, in "other" cultures, family, extended family, and peer support are more significant. Hence, the impact of these opposing values of the counselor and his or her mainstream society must be weighed constantly.

One assumes that the counselor of a person or persons exploring a transracial or interreligious marriage is more familiar with one of the two cultural backgrounds represented. The counselor can be coached and can learn from an "insider" or a trusted member of the less familiar cultural group. For example, a white counselor must watch his or her natural tendency to identify with the partner more acculturated to the counselor's dominant group. This can lead to triangulation or the alignment of the counselor and the counselee most like the counselor on one side and the more culturally different counselee on the other.

The counselor must understand his or her world view vis-a-vis the counselees' world views. A world view is defined as how a person perceives his or her relationship to our world. This includes all of the natural world, the social institutions, other people groups in the world, and a person's sense of responsibility toward a world full of nature, people, and social institutions. It includes attitudes, values, opinions, and concepts. For minorities in the United States, a world view includes the subordinate position assigned them by society and how that affects them in the areas of economics, social class standing, social life, and sexual and religious expression. Counselors should not be culture-blind, communicating only according to their own conditioned values, assumptions, and perspectives of reality without regard to other views.

A significant part of a counselor's and counselee's world view is the locus of control and locus of responsibility. The locus of control is perceived as internal or external—does the individual or his/her environment have ultimate control over what happens to him or her? The locus of responsibility can place the blame for whatever happens to a person on the individual or on factors in the individual's environment. Attitudes toward the ability of individuals to make changes in his or her situation are influenced by that individual's view of locus of control.

One culture-bound value is how, how quickly, and to what extent one gets to know a new person. How close should two individuals in various relationships, including marriage, become—either physically or emotionally? The measure of tolerated physical closeness can be related to expected emotional closeness. The counselee's expectations of emotional closeness or distance can also affect the counselor's interviewing style. How much personal information should acquaintances or counselors and counselees share? Careful observation and listening can give the counselor some clues concerning the degree of closeness the counselees expect.

Hall (1980) defines *intimate* physical space between two persons as varying from body contact to about 18 inches apart; *personal* space is from 18 inches to 4 feet; *social* distance is from 4 feet to 12 feet; and *public* space (distance for speeches and other formal communication) is more than 12 feet. People originally from third-world countries tend to expect more closeness in all of these categories.

Most counselors in the United States tend to assume that counseling is primarily directed toward the development and adjustment of individuals rather than units of individuals or groups such as the family or organizations. Some cultural groups in this society have more of a community focus.

Paul Pedersen (1987) posits ten assumptions of Western cultural bias that the white, dominant-society counselor should be aware of:

1. There is an implicit assumption "that the definition of

'normal' is more or less universal across social, cultural, and economic or political backgrounds." The more functional view is that what is "considered normal behavior will change according to the situation, the cultural background of a person or persons being judged, and the time during which a behavior is being displayed or observed" (17).

2.   Individuals are the "basic building blocks of society." The individual "criteria of self-awareness, self-fulfillment, and self-discovery are important measures of success in most counseling in Western society. . . . In Chinese culture it would be normal and natural to put the welfare of the family before the welfare of any individual member of that family" (18).

3.   Problems brought to counseling are defined "from a framework limited by academic discipline boundaries" (19). The counselee's cultural perspective may include ramifications of the problem that extend beyond the counselor's usual assessment parameters: Is the counselor-defined psychological problem really caused by non-adherence to traditional customs?

4.   Western culture depends on abstract words and counselors assume that counselees will understand these abstractions. Dominant society in the United States is a high-context culture (the meaning of concepts is dependent on reference to context). Many other cultures are low-context and are "more likely to presume that abstract concepts carry their own meaning with them from one context to another" (19).

5. Independence is "valuable and dependencies are undesirable. . . . If a counselor encounters 'excessive' dependency in a client, he or she is likely to see the elimination of that dependency as a desirable outcome for counseling. Yet, there are many cultures in which

dependencies are described as not only healthy but absolutely necessary" (20).

6. This assumption "relates to the perceived importance of natural support systems surrounding a client. Counselors need to endorse the potential effectiveness of family and peer supports to a client (21).

7. This assumption is that "everyone depends on linear thinking—wherein each cause has an effect and each effect is tied to a cause—to understand the world around them." But some cultures see cause and effect as "two aspects of the same undifferentiated reality. . ." (21).

8. Another assumption is that "counselors need to change individuals to fit the system and are not intended to change the system to fit the individual" (22).

9. This assumption "relates to the relevance of history for a proper understanding of contemporary events. Counselors are more likely to focus on the immediate events that created a crisis. . . . The client's perspective may require historical background knowledge that the client feels is relevant to the complete description of his or her problem from his or her point of view" (22-23).

10. The last assumption is that "counselors already know all of their assumptions. . . . All counseling is viewed to a greater or lesser extent, cross-cultural." Counselors must remain willing "to challenge [or have challenged] more of their unexamined assumptions about themselves and the world about them" (23).

These suggestions of ways of looking at oneself and looking at some possible pitfalls of unsubstantiated assumptions about less-known cultures can be helpful in preparation for sensitive counseling across cultures. The concerned counselor should realize his or her deficiencies in this area and should seek to constantly increase awareness and information. This should include awareness of one's own cultural limitations, openness to cultural differences, and a counseling style oriented to the counselee's culture.

Counselors should test the assumptions that are relevant in every cross-cultural counseling relationship. They can improve their readiness for such counseling by reading about counseling skills and treatment approaches for specific minority groups, reading recent ethnographic studies conducted by minority group researchers, and reading first-person accounts of growing up in a minority culture. The learner can also interview minority professionals, community leaders, the counselees themselves, and others who can represent a particular cultural group. Direct experience of minority-group activities, ceremonies, and community events are helpful in gaining trust and respect from a group, and in learning relevant aspects of the group's social life and organization.

Summary

The counselor brings to counseling a particular knowledge base, a set of values, and certain methods of counseling—all of which have been shaped in part by his or her own cultural background, by that of the dominant culture, and possibly by the values and ethics of a professional helping community.

Minority Model for the Development of Racial Identity

Sue and Sue (1990, 107-115) outline five stages that individuals pass through in the development of the racial identity part of their self-concept. Their paradigm closely parallels two other five-stage cultural awareness development models: one integrated and conceptualized by Christensen (1988), and another summarizing and integrating three models (Sabnani et al. 1991, 76-93). Sabnani et al. detail a number of exercises and experiences that can help a dominant-society counselor progress through the stages. All of the paradigms have one model for whites and another for non-whites or minorities. If the counselor can align him or herself with one of the stages in one of the models, he or she can understand better how the self is involved in relating to another culture. If the counselor belongs to the dominant culture and one or both of the counselees are members of a minority group, the counselor can help counselees position themselves in a stage of one of the scales and help determine what it takes for effective counselor-counselee and counselee-counselee relationships. The counselor must also be sensitive to the potentially changing and developing nature of an individual's cultural identity. Sue's five stages are aimed primarily at minority counselees, and run thus (Sue 1990, 66):

Minority Model

Conformity Stage. The counselee prefers and may become dependent on white counselors and is antagonistic toward minority counselors. Exploration of cultural identity is threatening. It may bring out dissatisfaction with one's personal appearance.

Dissonance Stage. The counselee is more open to self-exploration. He or she may prefer a white counselor but is more likely to choose a minority counselor because of some knowledge of the minority membership culture.

Resistance and Immersion Stage. In this stage, racism is the only legitimate area for exploration. Self-disclosure to whites is dangerous. There is a tendency to blame the Establishment for problems. Few in this stage use counseling. As a symbol of the establishment, the counselor is tested.

Introspection Stage. Counselees may prefer a same-race

counselor but may accept another counselor who understands a minority world view. There is some conflict between identity with their own group and independent attitudes. Will they be viewed as rejecting their own culture? Self-exploration moves them toward integrating and incorporating a new sense of identity.

Synergetic Articulation and Awareness Integrative Stage. In this stage, preference for counselors is not based on race but on acceptance of a world view.

White Racial Identity Stages

The stages suggested by Christensen (1989) are aimed primarily at majority counselors::

Conformity Stage. The person is ethnocentric with minimal awareness and limited knowledge of minorities. He or she holds many stereotypes for minorities and accepts white superiority and minority inferiority. The person is "not racist" but believes that minority inferiority justifies discrimination. Denial and compartmentalization result in differences being unimportant.

Dissonance Stage. The counselor can begin to deal with the inconsistencies. The person begins to see his or her own racism in conflict with non-racist philosophy, attitudes, and social programs. The person sees discrimination but rationalizes his/her powerlessness to change anything ("I'm only one person").

Resistance and Immersion Stage. The person becomes aware of universal racism and experiences shame and guilt over his/her own and group-racist practices (including family and friends). He/she can have negative feelings about being white and can assume the role of paternalistic protector of minorities or of over identification with a minority group (to escape whiteness).

Introspective Stage. After swinging from white identity to rejection of whiteness, the person becomes more autonomous and does not let either group define his or her whiteness. He/she is no longer controlled by guilt or anger, is less defensive, and no longer denies whiteness.

Integrative Awareness Stage. A non-racist white identity emerges. There is increased knowledge of institutional racism, appreciation for cultural diversity, and social commitment against racism.

Some cautions in using the model are these: The process of development through the stages is dynamic, the stages are not fixed, and a person can react to some things in one stage while reacting to other things in other stages.

VII

Premarital Counseling

Introduction

All couples planning marriage could benefit from premarital counseling. Many churches require counseling for the persons their pastors marry, and most ministers utilize some form of marriage education whenever possible. This present discussion and these suggestions for premarital counseling are geared to counselors, but they could be useful to the many others who, formally or informally, help prepare young people for marriage.

Goals and Purposes of Premarital Counseling

At the time most people considering marriage become receptive to counseling, they are well advanced in their courtship and have decided to get married. This can make rather difficult one of the general purposes of premarital counseling—to help those contemplating marriage determine whether or not they are mature and ready for marriage. They need to understand their strengths and weaknesses as individuals and as a couple. This timing complicates another purpose of premarital counseling—the exploration of areas of compatibility and the final determination of whether or not the two partners "fit" each other. Premarital counseling helps couples prepare for marriage. The term "counseling" as used in this book does not refer primarily to the amelioration of depth or long-term personality problems but to discussions geared to the purposes stated above.

This chapter first addresses briefly premarital counseling in general since it is assumed that any counselor who undertakes

73

mixed- marriage premarital counseling will have some knowledge of general premarital counseling.

Some Suggestions for Premarital Counseling

The couple planning marriage needs information, facts, ideals, and knowledge of the practical adjustments that are necessary for a successful marriage. Just as important is an understanding of the baggage that each partner brings to the relationship—the habit patterns and views, prejudices, and preferences that color one's expectations of marital behavior. The Christian counselor also needs to challenge the couple to the "building of a new unit in the present and eternal kingdom of God" (Methodist Pastors' Manual 1958, 22).

Counselors and counselees who value a biblical foundation for marriage might be guided by several texts which can also direct some relationships within marriage:

1. Genesis 1:27 supports God-given sexuality and the equality of the sexes.

2. Genesis 2:24 supports the primacy and permanence of the marital bond.

3. Ephesians 5:21-23 helps define the role of submission in marriage. (The author realizes that some see this submission as one-sided.)

4. 1 Corinthians 13 helps define love within and outside of marriage.

5. 1 Corinthians 7:1-5 gives a biblical basis for sexual activity within marriage.

These and such texts as Mark 10:9, Colossians 3:5-15, 1 Timothy 4:3-5, and 1 Peter 3:7 can provide material for fruitful discussions on the importance of marriage and proper attitudes and actions in marriage. All of the texts powerfully support the divine origin and nature of the marital relationship.

A number of writers have listed factors that seem to predict success in marriage. Two representative lists included here are presented to the counselor as guides for discussion of the couple's individual readiness for marriage and for their "fit" to each other. These must be applied to each situation and not used as absolute predictors of marital success or failure.

Some conditions and qualities that are related to success (Amstutz 1978, 97):

1. Happy family life (of the prospective marital partners) during childhood with good relations between father and mother, between parents and children.

2. Ability of the dating partner to have happy personal relations with peers and other significant persons such as teachers, relatives, and employers.

3. Completion of formal education. This involves the setting of goals and achieving them: intelligence, fitting in with society and its structures and goals.

4. Interest in family life, adjusting with reasonable comfort to traditional views, believing in reform to correct errors rather than resorting to destructive measures, hope for the future, love of children.

5. Commitment to mutuality and cooperation rather than independence and freedom.

6. Similar cultural and religious backgrounds.

7. Continued and deliberate courtship by personal choice and without premarital sex.

Exploration of the above areas can help marriage-bound

couples determine their strengths and weaknesses and the compatibility of their values as expressed in marriage.

The following variables are culled from the surveys of Lewis and Spanier (in Stahmann & Hiebert 1980, 11-12) and are based on research of healthy premarital couples:

1. The greater the premarital homogamy, or similarity in social and demographic factors, the higher the marital quality. The following emerge as predictors of marital stability or success: similarity of racial background, similarity of socioeconomic background, similarity of religious denominational affiliation, similarity of intelligence levels, similarity of age, and similarity of social status.

2. The specific premarital resources identified as predictive of quality and stability of marriage were: a high level of interpersonal skill-functioning, good emotional health, a positive self-concept, high educational level, an older age at first marriage, a high social class, a high degree of acquaintance before marriage, and physical health.

3. Marital quality and stability was correlated with high marital quality in the family origin, high level of happiness in one's childhood, and positive relationships between the person and his or her parents.

4. The fourth premarital variable category . . . is that of support from significant others. Predictive variables were parental approval of the future mate, the person's liking for the future in-laws, and the support of significant friends for the proposed marriage.

These variables of healthy marital partners and predictors of marital success paint an ideal picture of readiness for marriage. The counselor who helps a couple look at these should realize that a deviation from this ideal in one or two areas will not doom a marriage. However, serious thought and thorough discussion with couples and individuals should be given to any negative predictors and their possible future impact on marriage.

Scheduling Premarital Counseling

Fifty minutes has become the standard counseling interview period. This usually allows enough time to "warm up," catch up to where the previous session ended, work meaningfully on a few issues, and set the stage for the next session. But this length of interview is not sacred. The initial interview may include information gathering and may take an hour and a half or even two hours (especially for a couple). Scheduling and time constraints may dictate shorter interviews, and the cost of travel in time or money may lead to planned double sessions.

Since premarital counseling needs to cover a number of areas, even when the candidates are from similar backgrounds, it should consist of a minimum of five to seven interviews. The initial session and most of the rest should be with the couple jointly, but at least one should be with each candidate alone. The complexities of intermarriage may necessitate more sessions. Counseling needs are determined by the counselees' needs.

The counselor must be flexible concerning the number of counseling interviews. Some other variables which can affect the number are: the imminence of the wedding; the interests, time, and preparation of the counselor; and the readiness of the couple for counseling. Morris (1960, 18) mentions four levels of "readiness": (1) the emotionally mature who are in good emotional and physical health and are from wholesome homes, (2) immature or emotionally unstable individuals who already have maladjustments in their relationship with each other, (3) the physically sick or handicapped who need medical assessment along with counseling, and (4) the neurotic or psychotic who are unsuited to marriage but who might be helped by more traditional psychotherapy or counseling.

Content and Important Areas
in Premarital Counseling

The First Counseling Interview

The first interview ideally should be with both partners. It could have been initiated by either or both of them or by a minister. Presumably, at the time of the setting of the appointment, the couple would have been given background-information forms to fill out on themselves and their families (see Appendix A). This information is discussed in detail in the individual interviews and guides the counselor in this interview. The counselor outlines the proposed format for the sequence of sessions and the counselees "contract" the meeting times and places.

A discussion of wedding plans can help the counselor understand how this couple operates and may affect some of the arrangements discussed in the above paragraph. The first interview also should cover the individuals' church relationships or whatever other religious position each person holds.

Separate Interviews With Each Partner

The major purpose of the separate interviews is to provide a permissive atmosphere in which the interviewee may give freer expression to his or her feelings and objectively discuss perceived problems in the approaching marriage.

The background history questionnaire (Appendix A) is helpful in taking a careful look at the family of origin. The role of parents and significant others as models should be explained to help overcome any resistance to this "probing." Tracing the family tree seems to be a less anxiety-provoking way of approaching this discussion. The use of simple diagrams of family structure on a blackboard or piece of paper can be helpful.

The counselor can wrap up this in-depth look at family and background by summarizing and pointing out what was impressive or of concern.

In a personal interview, the counselor also can explore the counselee's understanding of maturity and evaluation of him or herself as emotionally mature. This can include typical reactions to frustration and tolerance of differences.

Covering the above material may take up to two interviews and, of course, needs to be repeated with the other partner.

Joint Interviews After the Individual Sessions

Many format options exist, and many lists of suggested premarital counseling topics to be covered in joint interviews are available. All of the lists seem to include the same few topics that most of the experts believe can be problematic in marriage or can help people develop the skills for communicating and coping. A more general topic to begin with could be "building the relationship." The subject headings of a few other significant topics for discussion are listed below. Comments and suggestions will be included for some of the topics.

Family Planning and Child Rearing

On a number of marital-satisfaction surveys, couples report less happiness in their marriage after children come. They, therefore, need to become realistic on the potential impact of adding children to their marriage. Potential partners can hold very divergent opinions on child-rearing practices (especially discipline), and on such things as birth control and ideal family size. The couple planning marriage may need a thorough understanding of each other's viewpoints. These viewpoints are strongly influenced by culture. The counselor needs to make sure that one partner has not submerged strongly held ideas just to reach agreement in some of these crucial areas. Such submerged ideas can surface later and cause painful conflict.

In-law Relationships

To some extent, in-law problems tend to be a part of all marriages. Since people marry families along with individuals, their relationships with in-laws belonging to different cultures may be especially problematic.

Social and Recreational Activities

Potential marriage partners' likes and dislikes, and "shoulds" and "oughts" are based on personal preferences, family traditions, and cultural prescriptions. Their differences in this area should be explored thoroughly and made explicit to both partners.

The Sexual Relationship

Sexual relationships is another area where culture and family covert and overt messages play a significant role in determining not only what is acceptable activity but what is acceptable communication concerning that activity.

Spiritual Activities

Religion can be a unifying force in the home, but it is most effective when both partners belong to the same church, attend regularly, and are active in church activities. Of course, the pastor or counselor should not pressure either partner to join a church, but could help the couple negotiate what will work out best when they represent different denominations or one is unchurched.

Family devotions may sound old-fashioned and when attempted are not always easy to fit into busy schedules. They can be at any time of the day and have no prescribed length or format. It is best when all who attend can participate, and worship can reflect everyone's choices of activities.

Hopefully, the premarital counseling experience will help bond the couple, and, if done by a pastor, give them a spiritual advisor and mentor during their marriage.

Communication

The counselor needs to help the partners understand each other's cultural filters that determine what is communicated and how it is communicated. Since much communication is implicit rather than explicit, and non-verbal rather than verbal, the partners need to learn to be patient, non-judgmental, and flexible in their communication.

Homework for Counselees

A number of counselors find it helpful to give counselees something to work on between interviews. Much of the desired growth or movement can take place as counselees explore and mull over things discussed in the most recent counseling session. Specific tasks assigned by the counselor can focus this growth. Counselees can be asked to read short articles or whole books that can be discussed in subsequent sessions. Some suggestions for assigned reading are found in Appendix B.

Another homework task can be the completion of a simple questionnaire by an individual or a couple. Such a questionnaire can help people become aware of feelings, can explore compatibility, or can help predict potential conflict areas in a relationship. Of course, these questionnaires are most helpful if the results are discussed with the counselor. Counselees also can be asked to list the pros and cons related to a given decision. They can be assigned other things to put in writing or they may want to work on a process of behavioral habit change at home (see Appendix C). Other homework assignments can include talking with someone with relevant experience, investigating community resources that can be helpful in establishing a mixed marriage, or simply thinking about an idea that arose in a counseling interview.

How and When to Make Referrals

Every counselor reaches a point with some counselees where someone else can be more effective in premarital counseling. It should be part of a counselor's skill development to learn to recognize and accept that need for change. The need for referral could be indicated by the counselee's prejudice against the counselor's membership group (or vice versa) that prevents an unbiased acceptance of the other person's communication. Sometimes the counselor realizes that someone else has more knowledge in a specific area or in the broader area in which counseling was sought. Another need for referral that must be sensitively assessed is when counseling reaches an impasse and it becomes obvious that no progress has been made for several interviews or the counselor is encountering too much resistance from the counselee(s) to make continuing with the same counselor profitable. Such resistance can be indirect and can be shown by broken appointments, tardiness, non-acceptance of the counselor's ideas, procrastination in homework, etc. Referral can mean either turning over the counseling to someone else or asking the counselee to make limited contacts with a third counselor while the initial counselor continues the regular counseling.

Summary

This chapter discusses some of the purposes, guidelines, and tools for cross-cultural premarital counseling. It includes some marital readiness criteria and some suggested topics for premarital counseling discussions.

VIII

Multicultural Counseling

As discussed in chapter 6, formal counselors, informal counselors, and even people who just pass on opinions need to know something about themselves and their attitudes. They need to know whether they can be objective and whether they are basing their communications on up-to-date cultural information. In addition, the counselor needs to know how best to help people make their own decisions. He or she should be as well equipped as possible to effectively help potential mixed-marriage partners with their serious, complex, but hopefully permanent decisions regarding their marriages.

Traditional Counseling

Since the United States is part of a Western-society world view, counseling tends to be a white, middle-class activity that holds many values and characteristics that are different from those of third-world (minority) groups. The traditional counselor role has been founded on what can further be described as a psychological world view. This view focuses on the individual and on traits and conditions of the individual.

Traditionally in counseling, individuals are treated primarily as independent entities, having identities all their own and problems bounded to a large degree by their individual identities. Individuals are viewed as having intelligence, skills, abilities, personality traits, interests, self-concepts, mental disturbances, adjustment disorders, etcetera (Cottone 1988 in Cottone 1991, 398).

In general, counseling programs are derived from, and serve to affirm, the values of American (dominant-society) culture. This approach to counseling is based on some common assumptions: linear causality (*A* causes *B* in a straightforward fashion), subject-object dualism (the observed and the observer are distinct), determinism (causes can be directly defined), individualism (the study of the individual predominates), and absolutivism (there is a universal non-relative reality). Obviously, these assumptions do not underlie the cultural belief systems of many of the non-dominant cultures discussed in chapter 2. Without sensitive consideration of diversity, socio-cultural variables are not acknowledged in counseling and the counseling becomes culturally insensitive.

Multicultural Counseling

In multicultural counseling, potential marriage partners coming for counseling belong to different cultures and the counselor often represents an additional culture. In fact, a counselor in the United States is most likely a member of the dominant, Western-European cultural group, and the counselees belong to minority groups. Therefore, premarital counseling for a couple entering a mixed marriage is multicultural counseling.

Multicultural counseling is that in which the counselor and client differ as a result of socialization in unique cultural or racial/ethnic environments. Multicultural counseling recognizes cultural diversity as a reality. It affirms diversity and pluralism as valuable, as something to be preserved and extended. Multicultural counseling values general human qualities, individual uniquenesses, and the influences of cultural group membership on both. (Ponterotto & Casas, 1987; Sue, 1981; Vontress, 1988 in Locke 1990, 18)

The multicultural counselor needs knowledge of the

counselees' culture and status, if possible, and experience with the counselees' cultural group. This increases his or her ability to devise innovative counseling strategies that relate to the unique counselee's needs. This counseling atmosphere is enhanced by the counselor's acceptance of the counselee as a cultural equal and the establishment of a relationship between two equivalent beings.

The counselor also should be aware of the potential impact of his or her cultural, ethnic, or racial background on the counselees. The difference between counselor and counselee backgrounds can be used as an excuse for the spouse-to-be feeling "outside" to withdraw from counseling. This can be dealt with by an open discussion and clarification of cultural differences during the first interview. The counselor may want to invite the counselees to express concern whenever they feel the counselor's cultural sensitivity is "slipping."

In a cross-cultural situation, how much knowledge of the "other culture" does the counselor need? Can an adequate cultural background be gained by reading? Does the counselor need to have lived in the area where the less-known culture is based? Is a knowledge of the history, art, literature, and general customs necessary? Or should he or she just try to gain an empathetic understanding of the more homely, intimate background details (Bolman 1969, 1239)? The counselor cannot know too much or be too sensitive.

A Model for Multicultural Counseling

Dillard (1983, 268) posits a counseling model that includes stages involving verbal and non-verbal transactions in successive interviews aimed at certain goals. Multicultural counseling goals must be viewed from two frames of reference: (1) they must assist culturally different clients to deal with their psychosocial environment; and (2) they must assist these clients in restructuring their environment to accommodate their personal and cultural needs. In other words, clients need to explore their feelings and attitudes, and their friends', relatives', and society's attitudes regarding a certain problem or plan. The clients may then need to change their social and physical situation and/or their plan or problem (with the counselor's help). The counselor can assist the culturally different client to adapt to or reshape his/her psychosocial environment.

Basic Skills of Culture

The counseling strategies to attain these goals include verbal and non-verbal counselor skills. These are: (1) basic skills focusing on patterns of culturally specific non-verbal behavior, (2) microcounseling skills focusing on culturally appropriate listening and influencing skills, (3) qualitative skills dealing with subjective dimensions that communicate understanding to the client in his/her own frame of reference, and (4) focus skills concentrating on the client or others as the prime subject of conversation. Effectiveness in this fourth area supports effectiveness in the other three areas. Two examples of non-verbal communication are eye contact and body language.

Eye Contact. The counselor should vary eye contact and not stare. However, too frequent breaks in eye contact may suggest to the client that the counselor is preoccupied, bored, inattentive, or unconcerned. Patterns of eye contact and the interpretation of it vary across cultures.

Body Language. Interpretation of body language varies between as well as within cultural groups. The counselor's interpretation of body movements should be geared to the cultural background of the client. Misinterpretation can lead to serious problems in communication.

Linked to body language is proximity or personal-space preference. The most comfortable physical distance between the client and the counselor varies within and between cultures.

Effective counseling is dependent on the counselor's

awareness of the appropriateness of certain subjects with clients of different cultural backgrounds. Needed here is extensive knowledge of the different groups. For example, sensitivity would be needed in discussing fatherless homes among blacks, and abortion among most Hispanics.

Microcounseling Skills

The microcounseling skills of closed-end questions, verbal encouragement, reflection of feelings, paraphrasing, and summarization are familiar to most counselors, so only a few comments on their application to multicultural counseling are given here. Members of some cultural groups may be reluctant to disclose or acknowledge the counselor's reflection of their feelings, especially early in the counseling relationship. Paraphrasing should be used with equal caution.

Influencing Skills

Influencing communication skills is one way the counselor helps the client. Communication skills include giving directions and expressing content, opinions, and advice. In cross-cultural counseling, these skills are used much as they are in same-culture counseling, but there should also be sensitivity to cultural variation.

Qualitative Skills

Qualitative skills are attempts to improve the quality of the counseling relationship by improving communication. These attempts include immediacy, confrontation, and genuineness. At times, it may be culturally inappropriate to use the direct "spotlight" skills of immediacy. Confrontation should be used guardedly because people in some cultures talk more figuratively and express information more indirectly. Genuineness is important in a cross-cultural situation; openness, authenticity, and honesty must be communicated to the client.

Focusing Skills

Cultures vary markedly in the determination of the appropriate focus for counseling. Flexibility should enable the culturally effective counselor to converse on many topics appropriate to the client and his/her culture. The focus can shift from self-focus to a focus on other persons, to a mutual or group focus, to a focus on various topics, or to a cultural-environmental focus. The counselor must be willing to shift the focus to other persons more frequently with minority clients. The cultural-environmental focus may be important in working with cultures that have experienced oppression and discrimination—the problem may be with society rather than within the individual.

The skills in the four above areas can guide the counselor in exploring feasibility and readiness for cross-cultural marriage.

Another Cross-Cultural Counseling Model

Green (in Fukuyama 1990, 11) describes a "'Help-Seeking Behavior' model which identified the following essential components in the client's culture: client problem recognition, labeling and diagnosis, utilization of indigenous helpers, and problem resolution according to client criteria." These roles of clients make the counseling activities relevant to the client's cultural background. These components form a model of multicultural counseling that can help make the counseling process sensitive to the cultures involved.

Cross-Cultural Attention to Stages of Counseling

Precounseling Stage

The counselor's eye contact with the counselee should be culturally suitable and should make the counselee comfortable. The counselee's avoidance of direct eye contact should be categorized as personal or cultural, and the seating should be arranged accordingly. Awareness of the counselee's interpretation of body positions is also important. The customary counselor-counselee physical juxtaposition may not be acceptable to many minority counselees.

The culturally skilled counselor must also interpret hand gestures and hand and eye movements. A gesture by an Asian American that would mean "come closer" to a typical American may actually mean "get away" (Ho in Dillard, 1983, 286). A counselee may be more attuned to a counselor's tone of voice than to his or her words. Thus, the counselor should adopt a positive tone of voice and not sound harassed, condescending, disinterested, or unpleasant. The counselor carefully should observe the counselee to note whether there is a need to adjust the counselor's rate of speech to facilitate communication. And the counselor's competence and/or right to discuss personal and cultural topics must be acceptable to the counselee.

First Counseling Stage: Self-Exploration

The counselee's exploration of feelings, emotions, and experiences can be encouraged by the counselor's warmth if it is attuned to the counselee's cultural understanding and personal readiness for warmth. Initially high levels of warmth can be counter productive to a client who has received little or no warmth or who has been taken advantage of. Other counselees may see an initial high level of counselor warmth as counselor weakness. In this initial stage, the counselor's concrete statements that focus on the counselee's specific feelings, behaviors, and experiences facilitate disclosure more than discussions of vague or intellectual topics.

Immediacy, or a focus on the "here and now," enhances the counselee's self-exploration. It can be conveyed by: (1) statements in the present tense ("right now your face is flushed"), (2) client assumption of responsibility using "I" statements ("I decided to stay home"), (3) helping counselees change vague or indirect responses to more direct expressions, and (4) helping the counselee avoid the use of vague modifiers such as "sort of," "maybe," "seldom," "perhaps," or "rather."

In this initial phase, the counselor can use confrontation to maintain open and sincere communication, deal directly with the issues, and point out differences among ideas, emotions, facts, and verbal and non-verbal behavior.

The second phase of the first stage involves a deeper exploration of feelings and emotions related to the counselee's personally relevant material. The counselor focuses on the counselee's emotional investment in his or her problem using empathy, reflection, paraphrasing, and summarization to mirror and bring into awareness the counselee's emotions.

Second Counseling Stage: Self-Understanding

In this stage, the counselor assists the culturally different counselee to reconstruct the communicative process and thereby understand his or her behavior and the behavior of others as it relates to the problem. The counselee is helped to clearly understand the problem before considering alternative courses of action. To achieve the above, the counselor uses influencing skills, is willing to give the counselee pre-counseling directions, and expresses some feelings in order to help the counselee do so. The counselor might contribute advice, opinions, or information. Other skills the counselor uses during this stage are interpretation and influencing summarization (combining self-expression of content and feeling).

The Third Counseling Stage: Action

Readiness for this stage is based upon the counselor's reaching a minimum level of understanding that permits him or her to make statements that demonstrate a basic understanding of the counselee's emotions and their meanings. The counselee now needs to develop and implement a strategy for actively altering or affecting the problem situation. First, concerns must be identified and immediate concerns ranked. Next, immediate concerns should be translated into clear, concrete goals and subgoals. Then the counselee should be helped to list alternative courses of action and gather relevant information. The counselee should then choose a course of action, take the action, and evaluate the action taken (Dillard 1983, 285-310).

Just the major points of the multicultural counseling process according to communication stages are included above.

The network approach to counseling has been used successfully with native-Americans. A clan, or a group of family, relatives, and friends, is organized and mobilized to form a social force or network that works to deal with alienation and the results of discrimination. The counselee and his or her problems are considered and treated within the context of a larger family and community social system. This is in keeping with a cultural tradition of reliance on group consensus in dealing with problems.

Practical Considerations in Applying Multicultural Counseling Models

Any attempt to provide culturally effective counseling requires a great deal of flexibility in counseling style and model(s). In almost all counseling processes, both content (facts) and emotions (feelings) must be addressed. The cultural experiences of some counselees may dictate an adjustment between content and emotions in the process model. In addition, the counselee's psychosocial environment or impacting social systems may be responsible for his or her problems, and counseling goals should be formulated accordingly. This possibility definitely should be considered when counseling minorities.

Summary

This chapter covers some goals, some ideas on scheduling, and some suggestions for premarital counseling. It includes important content areas and concludes with suggestions for counselees' homework and how to recognize the need for and how to make referrals.

IX

Cross-Cultural Premarital Counseling

Attitudes of the Counselor and the Public

The importance of the counselor's attitude toward intermarriage cannot be overemphasized. In fact, the ideal is when the counselor is not just neutral but actually believes that a mixed marriage can have the potential of a rich and rewarding relationship. The communication of this hope can encourage the counselees' trust and openness—essential ingredients of successful counseling. When the counselee is reassured that he or she is not making a foolish mistake, he or she is free to express concerns regarding perceived or real problems in the relationship. The role of the counselor is not to encourage or discourage intermarriage but to assist the counselees in making thoughtful, wise decisions.

The attitude of dominant society toward intermarriage is also important and should be addressed in counseling.

The dangers of the misperception regarding compatibility should not be underestimated in light of the possibility of "self-fulfilling prophecy" (Jussim, 1986). Interethnic couples are faced by public expectation that their marriages are particularly vulnerable. Internalization of this view would seem likely to worsen the character of the marital relationship and its ability to deal constructively with ongoing problems. As such, premarital counsellors would do well in aiding couples planning an interethnic marriage to cope with these public views at the outset (Bizman 1987, 397).

The counselor can provide a safe atmosphere where counselees can express their feelings of anger and alienation.

Suggested Approach to Counseling

Specific approaches to counseling should be guided by an awareness of differences that can be grouped under three headings: culture-bound values, class-bound values, and language variables. Culture-bound values include an individual or group focus of the culture, the mix and emphasis on verbal/emotional/ behavioral expressiveness of the culture, other communication patterns, and the expected degree of openness and intimacy. Class-bound values are of particular concern when one counselee represents a lower-class lifestyle while the other represents the middle class. Some language variables are discussed in chapter 2.

Other culture-bound values significant to the counseling situation are the extent to which verbal reasoning tends to be analytical/linear (cause and effect), and whether there is a clear distinction between mental and physical well-being.

Class-bound values can include a strict adherence to a time schedule (such as a 50-minute, once-a-week interview schedule), a preference for an ambiguous or unstructured approach to problems, and the importance of long-range goals or solutions. Language variables include the preference for, and facility in, the use of standard English and the value of verbal communication (Sue & Sue 1990, 34). Since the counselor and the culturally different counselee may have different class values, language factors, unique or common experiences such as discrimination, and different communication styles, they must utilize relevant counseling approaches and set appropriate goals.

The perceived or real differences between the two partners'

families and/or the two partners in income, education, or related lifestyles, the feelings of each partner about these differences, and their plans for bridging the possible gaps should be thoroughly explored.

Great individual, familial, and cultural variations may determine what roles husband and wife should play in a marriage. For example, what do the counselees understand by "head of the family?" How much affection should a husband show? May he shed tears? How independent should a wife be? Should she work outside of the home? May she initiate sexual intercourse? Definite class and ethnic biases enter into the answers to the above and many other questions concerning every day marital adjustment.

Empathy in Cross-Cultural Counseling

It is almost a given that a counselor needs empathy, especially when working cross-culturally. However, when counselees from different cultural backgrounds are preparing for union, their individual capacities for empathy are just as important.

Empathy is the capacity to see oneself in the other person's situation. Gordon Allport (in Augsburger 1986) has postulated eight levels of empathy that start with motor mimicry and end with mystical union. Of the eight levels, successful intercultural marriage especially could utilize characteristics from his steps 4 through 8:

4. Identification between persons. The similarities between persons are noted, and a feeling of common identity is shared.

5. Persons know how the other feels.

6. Persons are connected in a common emotional bond.

7. One senses the state of mind of the other and respects it fully as one's own. There is a sense of oneness and of joint personhood.

8. There is a mystical union and an empathetic sense of joint experiencing of spiritual oneness (29).

While the scale shows a progression toward unity, it also includes a continuing need for detachment and separation. It is this complex, dynamic blend of needs, especially as addressed in a multicultural setting, that can complicate cross-cultural premarital counseling.

Shame and Guilt Across Cultures

Contemporary Western psychology (which underlies dominant-society traditional counseling) is almost uniformly negative in defining and in evaluating the emotion of shame. But Eastern psychologists see it as an essentially healthy part of humanness. Thus Eastern-oriented cultures believe that to be ashamed of oneself, one must maintain a deep level of positive feelings about oneself (Augsburger 1986, 123).

Guilt is defined and experienced in most cultures, but it is much more of a controlling factor in some cultures than in others. In a culture controlled predominantly by guilt, controls are expected to be internal. The guilt is focused on the violation of specific prescribed behaviors, and anxiety and shame tend to be repressed or denied.

From a Western (internally controlled guilt) viewpoint, the Japanese sense of guilt appears to be rather sluggish. But the Japanese sense of guilt displays itself dramatically when the individual suspects that his/her actions will result in the betrayal of the group to which he/she belongs.

Counselor and Counselee Self-Disclosure

Self-disclosure may be the most important behavior in which a counselee engages during counseling (Berg and Wright-Buckley

1988, 377). Lack of client self-disclosure is one of the most important problems in mixed-race counseling. But counselor disclosure can function as an appropriate model. The counselor's disclosure also can help reduce interpersonal distrust. As a result of a counselor disclosing, counselees may be more likely to view counselors as open, approachable, easily knowable, and friendly, and to view the counseling situation as "safe." This, in turn, should make it more likely that they will risk disclosing themselves (378). In fact, the culturally different person may not open up until the counselor discloses first. The counselor may have to share some personal feelings to "get the ball rolling." Counselees need help in understanding patterns of self-disclosure in their mate's culture and in separating unique personal patterns from those that are culture based. Self-disclosure may be particularly difficult between dominant-culture workers and minority groups experiencing discrimination since it presumes a degree of trust which may not exist initially.

I realize that some counselors may see themselves as a "blank screen" so any personal disclosure would be inappropriate; my suggested disclosure would not include intimately personal information, but just enough revelation for a limited illustration of disclosure, such as feelings about some example of culture shock.

More Cultural Impact on Counseling

The degree of acculturation (movement into the dominant-society culture) of a minority group member must be taken into account when attempting to understand that individual's cultural preferences and practices. It is very natural that in an initial counseling session one asks questions concerning language preferences and social group contacts to assess where on the acculturation continuum a particular counselee stands.

The counselee's experience is an important source of information. In order to understand how an individual's cognitive

activities, such as valuing, judging, and emoting , interact with
the conditions of his or her life to form internal experiences, it is
important to know how each individual represents the world.

Since intermarriage is more complex than within-group
marriage, the counselor may want to suggest a longer-than-
average engagement. This allows the couple more time to process
feedback from friends and relatives concerning the proposed
marriage.

Here is a summary of some culture-related things that can
inform the counselor as he or she leads out in discussion of the
proposed marriage:

1.   Marrying across economic class lines has similar
potential for problems as does marrying across ethnic, racial,
or denominational divisions. Cinderella-rich man marriages
can work, but feelings about who has or does not have money,
and different lifestyle expectations, can cause problems.

2.   Children added to a family will bring changes, including
changes in the relationship of marital partners. Definitions
of how to bring children up properly are conditioned by each
partner's cultural background and family child-rearing
practices. The couple may choose to have one partner play a
leadership role in child rearing and the other partner play a
supportive role. Or they may be equally active in nurturing
and disciplining their children. Parents from widely
divergent cultural backgrounds will begin by almost talking
two different languages in communicating about
child-rearing.

3.   Relatives can have a significant impact on the success
and happiness of a mixed marriage. The couple should be
helped to relate to the relatives empathetically whether the
relatives accept the mixed marriage or not. Parents may see
the marriage as disobedience or disloyalty to the family, the

church, or the ethnic group. The marital couple should be counseled not to return anger-for-anger and to maintain the relationship with close relatives if at all possible. Fortunately, most parents who reject such a marriage, initially, do "warm up" in a few years and eventually accept the mixed grandchildren. The counselor should be willing to meet jointly with the counselees and significant relatives to share information and discuss their questions, and, hopefully, help them become more objective regarding the marriage.

4. Cultural and religious beliefs have a subtle effect on attitudes toward sex. In fact, they are strong determinants of how much sex is discussed, how much sexual activity besides intercourse is desirable, and what birth control is allowable, if any. The new couple should at least be helped to begin dialogue toward a mutually-satisfactory level of sexual communication.

5. Good communication, of course, is essential in all of the above areas, and in all other aspects of marriage. Because of greater complexity and more potential problems, mixed marriages need better communication than non-mixed. (They also need greater commitment and, probably, a longer engagement). "Spouses in an intermarriage will view, interpret, and express things differently. These differences are not to be interpreted as simply personal inadequacies or rejections, rather they can be golden opportunities for learning and enrichment. To turn a potential liability into an asset, we should always communicate clearly and earnestly with our partner" (Ho, 1984, p. 81).

Communication across cultures must be with the ears (hearing the real issue), with the eyes (interpreting eye, head, hand, and body actions), and with the mind (putting together what the eyes and ears have taken in). The goal is an objective approach and a non-judgmental attitude.

Some conclusions based upon studies of racial-cultural minorities are:

1.   Minority counselees respond better to directive than non-directive counseling approaches.

2.   Active, rather than passive, approaches are preferred.

3.   Most minority counselees seem to prefer a structured, explicit approach rather than an unstructured, ambiguous approach.

4.   Many minority counselees tend to want counselors who may disclose some of their own thoughts, attitudes, and feelings before or during the counseling process.

5.   Short-term, task-oriented styles of counseling may be ineffectual with counselees who feel that extended periods of time "just talking" is an appropriate way to enter a relationship.

6.   Reflection—reaching for feelings or asking for insights— may appear inappropriate or intrusive.

7.   Some ethnic groups, Asian-Pacific Americans for example, may view help-seeking as a shame-inducing process and are extremely reticent to disclose personal problems. They, therefore, prefer counseling limited to the problem and focused on the present and immediate future.

Baptiste (1984, 375) warns that what may look like a problem of cultural difference actually may be an attempt of one future spouse to duplicate and establish as the family's standards those behaviors (i.e., "mother tongue" or dietary preferences) that were dominant in his or her family of origin. The couple's difficulties in maintaining ties with relatives could be blamed unfairly on cultural differences. However, a major source of conflict for the couple after marriage is the blood relatives or relatives by marriage who oppose the marriage and, thereby, cause the "opposite" spouse to feel ostracized or isolated.

Of course, cultural differences can be a major cause of marital problems. Each partner brings to the marriage a set of expectations for what marriage should be. These expectations are heavily influenced by his or her ethnic, cultural, and religious background. This includes what each expects of himself or herself as a spouse, what each expects of his or her spouse, and what each expects from the union. The roles and responsibilities in running the home and nurturing each other that each assumes are "right" can differ according to cultural and ethnic backgrounds.

Intermarried couples potentially face greater difficulty because differences in values, customs, and traditions associated with different ethnic groups, races, and religions must be added to the normal differences in personality, social class, education, and life experiences. This can be a serious problem because each person tends to feel that his or her particular culturally ordained values are incontestably "right" and "true" and "best." Each culture tends to teach its particular value system as the most appropriate way to conduct one's life.

The counselor should prepare the potential marriage partners to deal with issues rather than with basic personalities when culturally based differences arise. This level of discussion should be less traumatic and is probably better focused on the real problem.

If marriage is seen as a transition (an event resulting in or signaling change), than a mixed marriage is a doubly mixed transition—the marriage part is anticipated and the expected norm; the mixed part is unanticipated, or the unusual part unplanned for by society. The impact of this transition is important to the individuals, the union, the family, the other social networks, and the community. Schlossberg (1984, 52) suggests that one way to measure this impact is to note the extent to which daily life is altered—the relationships, the routines, and the assumptions about self and world roles. The goal is to assess the degree of difference between the pre- and post- transition environments.

One can also measure the impact of a mixed marriage by using a "psychological distance map"—comparing interactions with significant others in the old (before intermarriage plans became known or intermarriage occurred), and the new (the relatives and close friends now) environments. Counselor and counselee(s) can discuss the intensity and frequency of social contacts and assess the changes in social distance between the subject and his/her relatives and close friends. The marital transition process is an adaptation or alteration of life and behavior which should result in a stable new life organization or new identity *which may or may not be adequate* for the well-being of the individuals involved.

How does one know when a couple has worked through or can work through these changes and stabilize their lives in a new configuration? To help determine when their goal has been reached, the counselor can explore the impact of three major sets of factors that shape individuals in a mixed-marriage transition: (1) the variables that characterize the mixed marriage itself, such as the cultural differences; (2) the variables that characterize the particular individuals such as their personalities, their priorities and special interests, and their usual coping strategies; and (3) the particular environment which includes the supports that they have relied on, and the available supports if more or different ones become needed. The counselor must help the counselees balance their assets and liabilities in all three of the above areas.

Some of the other questions that need to be weighed in counseling are: what is the motivation for this mixed marriage and where did it come from? Are recent role changes partial causes of this mate choice (such as a divorce, geographical move, or new occupation)? Is related previous experience part of the background for the choice (such as knowledge of similar marriages)? Are the participants currently under a lot of stress?

Use of Support Groups

Support groups such as family, friends, and workplace associates fulfill basic human needs such as emotional support and the need to share feelings and explore problems with people who are known and trusted. Some minority groups in the United States rely more on extended families than does the dominant society. Persons who have chosen out-group marriage sometimes lose, at least temporarily, some of their social and emotional support systems. Counselors might encourage the individuals to join or help them to organize peer or self-help support groups. It is estimated that at least 500,000 such groups exist in the United States (Pedersen 1985, 88). These groups arise to meet a particular need such as adjusting to the loss of a spouse or facing the trauma of reaction to intergroup marriage. They are led by persons who have suffered and recovered from the malady or problem, and they emphasize non-formal counseling through nonprofessional volunteers. They also help through universalization—the knowledge that one is not alone; others are in the same situation and deal with the same feelings. Networks of acquaintances in the workplace also can serve as informal support systems.

The assumption that helpful supportive relationships must be nurturant is open to question. A caring and loving relationship may be helpful to a person in distress, but other types of relationships can provide information, guidance, feedback, and even laughter.

Dealing With the Culturally Determined Positions of Women Vis-a-vis Men

Modern counselors have an awareness of sexism and its negative impact on women and men. As a result of this concern, counseling as it is generally practiced in the Western world and dominant United States society tends to be geared to combat sexism. Therefore, any attempts to eliminate immediately all sex-biased values of one's culture from the relationships of the counselees is neither fully possible nor desirable.

Nonsexist Western counseling has as its goal the ability of the counselee to claim equality as an individual within the larger society. However, in cultures with their roots in the other two-thirds of the world where persons develop a family identity rather than a personal identity, the counseling mode should be more relational, familial, and group-process oriented. (The counselor may need a definition of sexist counseling such as is found in Augsburger (1986, 232-233).) Feminist counseling, on the other hand, tends to be too political and too disruptive of the social order for many minority cultures.

In summary, counselors are needed who have a profound understanding of the differences in the life cycle, life roles, and life possibilities of males and females within his or her culture of origin and in the culture of the counselee. Counselors need to help counselees explore gender assumptions that reflect sexism differentially in the two cultures represented. To enter into cross-cultural and cross-sex-role counseling at the same time requires knowledge, sensitivity, and skill.

Summary

Statistics on interracial marriage in the United States show that they account for less than 2% of all marriages, but the numbers are increasing. Some personality dynamics of persons who enter into such marriages include more advanced age and greater independence. Definitions of some terms commonly used in discussions on mixed marriages should help those with limited sociological backgrounds. Also discussed is the potential impact of prejudice and ethnocentrism on counselors, potential marriage partners, and the societal environment.

Immediate and long-term adjustments to interfaith and inter-denominational marriage are considered along with various denominational positions in mixed marriages. A biblical view of mixed belief systems in marriage is presented. It includes texts often used to justify racial prejudice.

The children of mixed marriages face some identity development problems but do not have significantly greater or deeper problems than children of same-race marriages. Emphasis in literature is divided between those who feel that children of black-white unions should be raised as black children and those who feel they should be considered biracial.

The counselor should be an individual who is not against interracial or otherwise mixed marriages and who knows his or her own prejudices. The counselor also should take into account the possible biases of one or both counselees.

Premarital counseling should help the partners determine the feasibility of the proposed marriage and guide them toward making the marriage a success. Of course, in a mixed marriage, the counseling process is compounded by cultural differences, societal attitudes, and ignorance of what to expect in marriage.

The book includes some topics and content for premarital counseling discussions and some cross-cultural models for the counseling process. It covers some pitfalls and guidelines for cross-cultural counseling and some body language and other expressions that are interpreted differently in different cultures.

It concludes with some reading, counseling homework, and a questionnaire in appendices.

My fond hope is that this volume will make the counselor's work a little easier and some mixed marriages a little happier.

Recommended Reading
For Counselees

For Mixed Marriages

Ho, Man Keung. (1984). *Building a Successful Intermarriage Between Religions, Social Classes, Ethnic Groups, or Races.* St. Meinrad, IN: Abbey Press.

Tannen, Deborah. (1990, December). Can't We Talk? (Understanding the Different Languages Men and Women Speak Can Keep Sparks From Flying). *Reader's Digest*, p. 19.

How Intermarriages Affect Children. (1984, August). *USA Today*, p. 5.

You Can't Join Their Clubs: Six Mixed Couples Get Together to Talk About Love, Marriage, and Prejudice. (1991, June 10). *Newsweek*, p. 48.

Interdenominational and Interfaith Marriage

Marget, Madeline. (1988, September 23). Madeline & Ernie: Honoring What We Do Not Share. (Jewish-Catholic Marriage). *Commonweal*, p. 491.

Witkin, Georgia. (1986, September). Odd Couples; Interfaith Marriages: Common, But Still No Piece of Cake. *Health*, p. 77.

Schumer, Fran. (1990, April 2). Star-Crossed: More Gentiles and Jews Are Intermarrying—and It's Not All Chicken Soup. *New York*, p. 32.

Interracial Marriage

Yudkin, Marcia. (1991, October 20).   Chen's Mother. (Intercultural Marriage). *The New York Times Magazine*, p. 22.

Kantrowitz, Barbara. (1988, March 7).   Colorblind Love: One Group of Friends Still Lives the Dream (Black and White in America). *Newsweek*, p.40.

Carter, Richard G. (1991, August 4).   Weathering Prejudice. (Personal Narrative of an Interracial Marriage). *The New York Times Magazine*, p. 14.

Norment, Lynn. (1985, September).   A Probing Look At the Children of Interracial Marriages: Do They Have the Best of Both Worlds or Are They 'Catching It' from Both Sides? *Ebony*, p. 156.

Appendix A

Premarital Counseling Questionnaire

Name _____Date _____

Present Address _____

Permanent Address _____

Be sure to answer every question. Please put a check mark where called for. Do not check more than one alternative unless asked to do so. If not engaged or married, ignore "partner" questions.

1. Gender: ____ Male ____ Female

2. Race: ____ White ____ Black ____ Asian ____ Other

3. Age: Years ____ Months ____

4. Birthplace:
    ____ Inside U.S.A.
       Which state? _____
    ____ Outside U.S.A.
       Which country? _____
    ____ Do not know

5. Marital Status:
    ____ Single, not engaged
    ____ Single, engaged or going steady
    ____ Married
    ____ Widowed
    ____ Separated or divorced
    ____ Other (i.e., living together)

6. If Married:
    Date of your marriage: Month____ Date____ Year____
    How many children? ____
    Children's birthdates and gender:

    _____   _____
    _____   _____
    _____   _____
    _____   _____
    _____   _____

7. Birthplace of Parents:
    Father: **Mother**:
    ___ Born inside USA   ___ Born inside USA
    ___ Born outside USA   ___ Born outside USA
        Country _____   Country _____
    ___ Do not know   ___ Do not know

8. Any military service?
    Yourself: **Partner**:
    ___ Yes   ___ Yes
    ___ No   ___ No
    Date of entering: Date of entering:
    Date of discharge: Date of discharge:

9. What was the longest period you lived in one residence before you were 21? _____ years

10. In what religion were you and your partner brought up?

	You	**Partner**
Protestant	_____	_____
Jewish	_____	_____
Roman Catholic	_____	_____
Other_____	_____	_____
No organized religion	_____	_____
Do not know	_____	_____

11.   What is your religion and what is your partner's religion at the present time?

Religion	You	Part-ner
Protestant but not active		
Protestant and active		
Protestant and very active		
Catholic but do not attend		
Catholic and attend occasionally		
Catholic and devout		
Jewish but do not attend		
Jewish and attend High Holidays		
Jewish and attend regularly		
Other (not active)_____		
Other (active)_____		
Other (very active)_____		
No organized religion		
Do not know		

12. Give the alternative which best describes the number of years of school or college which you have completed and which your partner has completed. Include any vocational training such as nursing, secretarial, etc.

Years of School	You	Part-ner
8 years or less		
9 or 10 years (1 or 2 years of high school)		
11 or 12 years (3 or 4 years of high school)		
13 or 14 years (1 or 2 years of college)		
15 or 16 years (3 or 4 years of college)		
17 and over (postgraduate or professional education)		
Do not know		

13. Are you now a student?
    ___ Yes ___ No   Name of Institution:_____

14. Did you share in the housework when you were growing up?
    ___ No   ___ Yes, occasionally   ___ Yes, frequently

15. Do you like domestic activities now?
    _____ Like very much
    _____ Like somewhat
    _____ Slight dislike
    _____ Considerable dislike

16. In general, what activities do you participate in at the present time? Check one of the three columns for each of the following activities:

Activities	Never/ Seldom	Some- times	Often
TV or videos			
Movies away from home			
Dances			
Competitive sports (tennis, etc.)			
Spectator sports			
Outdoor activities (walking, riding, fishing, etc.)			
Social gatherings with friends (to play cards, talk, etc.)			
Reading			
Art appreciation (visiting art exhibits, play-going, music, etc.)			
Creative and interpretative art (writing, drawing, acting, singing, etc.)			
Politics			
Hobbies (collecting, mechanics, wood-work, needlework, etc.)			
Membership in clubs and organizations (school or college, national)			
Business or professional activities (beyond office hours)			

17. When you were 16 or 17 years of age, how many boy companions did you have?

_____ None or few   _____ Fair number   _____ Many

18. When you were 16 or 17 years of age, how many girl companions did you have?

_____ None or few   _____ Fair number   _____ Many

19. Occupational classification of your father as you were growing up (or of the man who supported the family):

_____No employment history

_____Unskilled worker

_____Semi-skilled worker (garage attendant, bench hand, farm hand, etc.)

_____Skilled worker (automobile mechanic, toolmaker, draftsman, police, firefighter, etc.)

_____White collar worker (file clerk, typist, salesperson, secretary, bookkeeper, clerk, etc.)

_____Small business man (retailer, garage operator, etc.)

_____Professional worker (teacher, minister, doctor, lawyer, artist, musician, army officer, etc.)

_____Business executive or professional administrator

_____Farmer

_____Not applicable (brought up in institution, etc.)

20. Occupational classification of your mother as you were growing up (or of the person who helped support the family):

_____No employment history

_____Unskilled worker

_____Semi-skilled worker (garage attendant, bench hand, farm hand, etc.)

_____Skilled worker (automobile mechanic, toolmaker, draftsman, police, firefighter, etc.)

_____White collar worker (file clerk, typist, salesperson, secretary, bookkeeper, clerk, computer operator, etc.)

_____Small business person (retailer, garage or beauty shop operator, etc.)

_____Professional worker (teacher, minister, doctor, lawyer, artist, musician, army officer, etc.)

___Business executive or professional administrator

___Farmer

___Not applicable (brought up in institution, etc.)

21. What is your occupational classification at this time?
(Specify the exact title of your job here and check the appropriate classification below.)_____

___Not employed for compensation (circle here for housewife, student, retired, etc.)

___Unskilled worker

___Semi-skilled worker (garage attendant, bench hand, farm hand, etc.)

___Skilled worker (automobile mechanic, toolmaker, draftsman, police, firefighter, etc.)

___White collar worker (file clerk, typist, salesperson, bookkeeper, secretary, clerk, etc.)

___Small business person (retailer, garage or beauty operator, etc.)

___Professional worker (teacher, minister, doctor, lawyer, artist, musician, army officer, etc.)

___Business executive or professional administrator

___Farmer

22. What is the present marital status of your own parents? Be sure to check only one.

___Married

___Separated (because of marital friction)

___Divorced, neither remarried

___Divorced, father remarried

___Divorced, mother remarried

___Divorced, both remarried

___Widowed, not remarried

___Widowed, remarried

___Neither living

___Other

23. If your own mother is living, check here_____. If your own mother is not living, how old were you when she died?_____

24. If your own father is living, check here_____. If your own father is not living, how old were you when he died?_____

25. If your own parents are not separated or divorced, check here ___. If your own parents are separated or divorced, how old were you when this occurred?_____

26. How would you describe your own parents' relationship to each other? (Or the relationship of the adults with whom you grew up?)
    ___Warmly affectionate and demonstrative
    ___Affectionate but reserved
    ___No signs of affection
    ___Not applicable (Comment_____)

27. To what extent were your parents in disagreement (or the adults with whom you grew up)?
    ___In conflict all of the time
    ___Alternately fighting and making up
    ___Tolerated each other without conflict
    ___No conflict apparent
    ___Do not know
    ___Not applicable

28. Appraisal of the happiness of your own parents' marriage (or the adults with whom you grew up):
___Very happy
___Happy
___Unhappy
___Very unhappy
___Do not know
___Not applicable

29. In the family in which you were raised, were there children other than yourself?
___No other children
___Yes (specify number irrespective of whether they are now living or not_____)

30. List the present ages of living brothers and sisters
Brothers   ___   ___   ___   ___   ___   ___
Sisters   ___   ___   ___   ___   ___   ___

31. What was your position among your brothers and sisters, according to order of birth? (Include all other children raised in your household.)
___Only child   ___Youngest child
___Oldest child   ___Intermediate child

32. On the whole, while you were growing up, how happy were you?

Before your teens	**During your teens**
___Very happy	___Very happy
___Happy	___Happy
___Unhappy	___Unhappy
___Very unhappy	___Very unhappy

33. How did you get along with your own mother?

Before your teens	**During your teens**	**At present time**
___Very well	___Very well	___Very well
___Fairly well	___Fairly well	___Fairly well
___Poorly	___Poorly	___Poorly
___Cannot say	___Cannot say	___Cannot say

(Cannot say–mother not living or did not have contact with her in this period).

34. How did you get along with your own father?

Before your teens	**During your teens**	**At present time**
___Very well	___Very well	___Very well
___Fairly well	___Fairly well	___Fairly well
___Poorly	___Poorly	___Poorly
___Cannot say	___Cannot say	___Cannot say

(Cannot say–father not living or did not have contact with him in this period).

35. Did you get along better with one parent than the other?

Before your teens
___Got along better with mother or her substitute
___Got along better with father or his substitute
___Got along with both parents equally well
___Not applicable

During your teens
___Got along better with mother or her substitute
___Got along better with father or his substitute
___Got along with both parents equally well
___Not applicable

At present time
___Get along better with mother or her substitute
___Get along better with father or his substitute
___Get along with both parents equally well
___Not applicable

36. Was your home with your own parents broken by death, divorce, or separation?

    ___Yes

    ___No

IF YOU ANSWERED "NO" TO THE ABOVE QUESTION (36), THE REMAINING QUESTIONS DO NOT APPLY TO YOU; THEREFORE, DO NOT ANSWER THEM UNLESS YOUR RESPONSE WAS "YES."

37. If your home was broken (you answered yes to question 36), with whom did you live afterward?

    ___Lived with father

    ___Lived with mother

    ___Lived with relatives other than father and mother

    ___Lived in institution

    ___Lived alone (boarding house, etc.)

    ___Other (specify)_____

38. If one of your parents remarried before you were 21, and you lived with that parent during that period, give your appraisal of the happiness of the remarriage.

    ___Not applicable

    ___Very happy

    ___Happy

    ___Unhappy

    ___Very unhappy

    ___Do not know

39. If you have lived with a stepmother, foster mother, or adoptive mother, how did you get along with her?

Before your teens	During your teens	At present time
___Not applicable	___Not applicable	___Not applicable
___Very well	___Very well	___Very well
___Fairly well	___Fairly well	___Fairly well
___Poorly	___Poorly	___Poorly

40. If you have lived with a stepfather, foster father, or adoptive father, how did you get along with him?

Before your teens	During your teens	At present time
___Not applicable	___Not applicable	___Not applicable
___Very well	___Very well	___Very well
___Fairly well	___Fairly well	___Fairly well
___Poorly	___Poorly	___Poorly

Questionnaire used by permission of the publisher. (Some modification by Reger C. Smith.)

From *Premarital Counseling: A Manual for Ministers* by Kenneth J. Morris, 1960, Englewood Cliffs, New Jersey: Prentice-Hall, Inc.

Appendix B

Cultural, Ethnic, and Religious Sensitivity Inventory

Here are some statements made by marriage counselors who work with intermarried couples. How often do you feel this way when you work with intermarried couples?

Circle one number for each statement. *Answer every question.*

In work with married couples, I . . .	Always	Fre-quently	Occasi onally	Seldom	Never
A. Realize that my own cultural/ ethnic/religious background may affect my effectiveness.	5	4	3	2	1
B. Make an effort to assure privacy and/or anonymity.	5	4	3	2	1
C. Am aware of the systemic sources (racism, poverty, and prejudice) of their problems.	5	4	3	2	1
D. Assist them in under-standing whether the problem is of an individual or of a collective nature.	5	4	3	2	1
E. Am able to engage them in identifying major progress in understanding.	5	4	3	2	1
F. Consider it an obligation to familiarize myself with their culture, ethnicity, and religion.	5	4	3	2	1

In work with married couples, I . . .	Always	Fre-quently	Occasi onally	Seldom	Never
G. Am able to understand and "tune in" to the meaning of their cultural/ ethnic/religious dispositions, behaviors, and experiences.	5	4	3	2	1
H. Am aware that some tech-niques are too threatening to them.	5	4	3	2	1
I. Am able at the termination to help them consider alternative sources of support.	5	4	3	2	1
J. Am sensitive to their fear of racist or prejudiced orienta-tions.	5	4	3	2	1
K. Consider the implications of what is being suggested in relation to each client's cultural/ethnic/religious reality (unique dispositions, behaviors, and experiences).	5	4	3	2	1
L. Am aware that lack of pro-gress may be related to culture, ethnicity, or religion.	5	4	3	2	1
M. Am able to encourage them at the end of counseling to share their satisfactions or regrets.	5	4	3	2	1

Used by permission of the author and publisher. Adapted and abridged by Reger C. Smith. From *Building a Successful Intermarriage Between Religions, Social Classes, Ethnic Groups, or Races* by Man Keung Ho, 1982, St. Meinrad, Indiana: Abbey Press.

Appendix C

Changing Habitual Behavior

How a person asserts himself or herself, expresses affection, or reacts to criticism, are all habitual ways of behaving that the individuals practiced, perhaps, from as far back in life as before puberty.

Most of an individual's reactions and emotional expressions are typical for that person; he or she has responded similarly over and over again. These responses (i. e., ways of handling anger or dealing with loss) have become habitual and are not easy to change. But following is a suggested routine for changing negative, habitual behavior patterns:

1. A person should decide on a specific, habitual behavior that should be changed and that he or she is willing to change.

2. If possible, this admission of need for change and decision concerning what will be worked on should be shared with someone close.

3. Once each day, the habit-changer should check up on himself or herself: "How well am I succeeding in my efforts to change?" "Can I think of specific examples of success in eliminating the undesired behavior or increasing the desired behavior?" "When will be the next opportunity for me to demonstrate the change I want to make?"

4. The brief check-up on progress (3 above) should be done at least once a day. It is repeated, brief attention to changing behavior that is effective.

5. At least once a week, the person confided in should be

contacted for his or her assessment of progress. The confidant should be honest about success or the lack of it and should be very supportive of any progress.

6. If this program of repeated effort and attention to behavior change is maintained consistently for at least a month, close friends may notice a difference in behavior and it will require less effort for the habit changer to practice the changed behavior.

7. If the above program is maintained for at least two months, the undesirable habit will lose its power and more desirable behavior will begin to replace it (as habit).

Bibliography

Abad, V., et al. (1974). A Model of Delivery of Mental Health Services to Spanish. *American Journal of Orthopsychiatry*, 44, 584.

Abney-Guardado, Armando J. (1983). *Chicano Intermarriage in the United States*. Unpublished Dissertation, Notre Dame, South Bend.

Allport, Gordon (1964). *Interracial Marriage*. Boston: Beacon Press.

Amstutz, H. Clair (1978). *Marriage in Today's World*. Scottdale, PA: Herald Press.

Arrendondo-Dowd, Patricia M., & Gonsalves, John (1980). Preparing Culturally Effective Counselors. *Personnel and Guidance Journal*, 58, 657.

Atkinson, Donald R., Morten, George, & Sue, Derald Wing. *Counseling American Minorities*. Dubuque, IA: William C. Brown.

Augsburger, David W. (1986). *Pastoral Counseling Across Cultures*. Philadelphia: Westminster Press.

Bahr, Howard M. (1981). Religious Intermarriage and Divorce in Utah and the Mountain States. *Journal for the Scientific Study of Religion*, 20, 251.

Baptiste, D. A., Jr. (1984). Marital and Family Therapy withRacially/Culturally Intermarried Step-families: Issues and Guidelines. *Family Relations*, 33, 373-380.

Bean, F. D. (1976). Intermarriage and Unwanted Fertility in the United States. *Journal of Marriage and the Family*, 38, 61.

Beaupere, Rene, & Piere-Yves, Emery (1969). *Marriages Mixtes*. Paris: Maison Marne.

Benson, Susan (1981). *Ambiguous Ethnicity: Interracial Families in London*. London: Cambridge University Press.

Berg, John H., & Wright-Buckley, Carol (1988). Effects of Racial Similarity and Interviewer Intimacy in a Peer Counseling Analogue. *Journal of Counseling Psychology, 35*, 377.

Bizman, Aharon (1987). Perceived Causes and Compatibility of Interethnic Marriage: An Attributional Analysis. *International Journal of Intercultural Relations, 11*, 387-399.

Blau, P. M., et al. (1982). Heterogeneity and Intermarriage. *American Sociological Review, 47*, 45.

Blau, Peter M., Beeker, Carolyn, & Fitzpatrick, Kevin M. (1984). Intersecting Social Affiliations and Intermarriage. *Social Forces, 62*, 585.

Bolman, M. (1968). Cross-Cultural Psychotherapy. *American Journal of Psychiatry*, 124, 1237.

Brandell, Jerrold R. (1988). Treatment of the Biracial Child: Theoretical and Clinical Issues. *Journal of Multicultural Counseling and Development, 16*, 176-187.

Broderick, Calfred B. (1979). *Marriage and the Family*. Englewood-Cliffs, NJ: Prentice-Hall.

Brownlow, W. G. (1862). *Sketches of the Rise, Progress, and Decline of Secession*. Philadelphia: George W. Childs.

Cazares, R. B. (1984). Mexican-American Intermarriage. *Social Science Quarterly, 65*, 626.

Chang, T. (1974). The Self-Concept of Children of Ethnically

Different Marriages. *Journal of Educational Research,* 25:245-253.

Christensen, Carole Pigler (1989). Cross-Cultural Awareness Development: A Conceptual Model. *Counselor Education and Supervision, 28,* 270-289.

Christiansen, Edward W. (1977). When Counseling Puerto Ricans. *Personnel and Guidance Journal, 55,* 412.

Coriden, James A., Green, Thomas J., & Heintschel, Donald E. (1985). *The Code of Canon Law: A Text and Commentary.* New York: Paulist Press.

Cottone, R. Rocco (1991). Counselor Roles According to Two Counseling Worldviews. *Journal of Counseling and Development, 69,* 398-401.

Cretzer, Gary A., & Leon, Joseph J. (Eds.). (1982). Intermarriage in the United States. *Marriage and Family Review, 5,* 3.

Croog, S. H., & Teele, J. E. (1972). Religious Identity and Church Attendance of Sons of Religious Intermarriage. *American Sociological Review, 32,* 93.

Cuellar, Ralph G. (1980). *Personality Traits and Interests in Thinking Related to Expressed Acceptance of Self and Others.* Thesis. Houston: University of Houston.

Das, Ajit K., & Littrell, John M. (1989). Multicultural Education for Counseling: A Reply to Lloyd. *Counselor Education and Supervision, 29,* 7.

Dillard, John M. (1983*). Multicultural Counseling.* Chicago: Nelson-Hall.

Duffy, Lorraine K. (1978). *The Interracial Individual's Self-concept, Parental Interraction, and Ethnic Identity.* Unpublished Masters Thesis. Honolulu: University of Hawaii.

Erikson, E. (1963). *Childhood and Society* (2nd ed). New York: Ed. Norton.

Fukuyama, Mary A. (1990). Taking a Universal Approach to Multicultural Counseling. *Counselor Education and Supervision, 30*, 6-17.

Gibbs, Jewelle Taylor (1987). Identity and Marginality: Issues in the Treatment of Biracial Adolescents. *American Journal of Orthopsychiatry, 57* (2), 265-278.

Giles, Hollyce C. (1990). Counseling Haitian Students and Their Families: Issues and Interventions. *Journal of Counseling and Development, 68*, 317.

Gim, R., Atkinson, D., & Whiteley, S. (1990). Acculturation and Willingness to See a Counselor. *Journal of Counseling and Psychology, 37* (3), 281.

Glenn, N. D. (1982). Interreligious Marriage in the United States. *Journal of Marriage and the Family, 44*, 555.

Glick, Clarence (1970). Interracial Marriage and Admixture in Hawaii. *Social Biology, 17*, 278.

Goldstein, Jay, & Segall, Alexander (1985). Ethnic Intermarriage and Ethnic Identity. *Canadian Ethnic Studies, 17* (3), 60.

Gordon, A. (1964). *Intermarriage. . . .* Hartford, CT: Greenwood Press.

Graybill, Ronald D. (1970). *Ellen G.White and Church Race Relations*. Washington, D. C: Review & Herald Publishing.

Gunthorpe, W. (1978). *Skin Color Recognition, Preference, and Identification in Interracial Children: A Comparative Study. Dissertation Abstract International.* 38(10-B) 3468.

Gurak, Douglas T., & Filzpatrick, Joseph P. (1982). Intermarriage Among Hispanic Groups. *American Journal of Sociology, 87*:921-934.

Hall, C. (1980) *Ethnic Identity of Racially-Mixed People: A Study of Black-Japanese*. Unpublished dissertation. Los Angeles: UCLA.

Hendrick, Susan S. (1988). Counselor Self-Disclosure. *Journal of Counseling and Development, 66*, 419.

Heer, David M. (1966). Negro-White Marriages in the United States. *Journal of Marriage and the Family, 28*, 262.

Hill, M., & Peltzer, J. (1982). Report on Thirteen Groups of White Parents for Black Children. *Journal of Family Relations, 31*, 557.

Ho, Man Keung (1984). *Building a Successful Intermarriage Between Religions, Social Classes, Ethnic Groups, or Races*. St. Meinrad, IA: Abbey Press.

Hobbs, Donald A., & Blank, Stuart J. (1978). *Sociology and the Human Experience*. New York: John Wiley & Sons.

Hurley, Michael (1975). *Beyond Tolerance*. London: Geoffrey Chapman.

Ibrahim, Farah A. (1985). Effective Cross-Cultural Counseling and Therapy: A Framework. *The Counseling Psychologist, 13*, (4), 625.

Idowu, Adeyemi I. (1985). Counseling Nigerian Students in United States Colleges and Universities. *Journal of Counseling and Development, 63*, 506.

Imbiorski, Walter J., & Thomas, John L. (1971). *Beginning Your Marriage*. Chicago: Delaney Publications.

Ivey, Allen E. (1987). Cultural Intentionality: The Core of Effective Helping. *Counselor Education and Supervision,*

Vol. 26 (March):168-172.

Ivey, Allen, Shizuru, Lanette, & Pedersen, Paul (1981). *Issues in Cross-Cultural Counseling* (Video). Amherst, MA: Microtraining Associates.

Jacobs, J. (1978). Black-White Interracial Families: Marital Process and Identity Development in Young Children. *Dissertation Abstracts International.* 38(10-B)5023.

Jansen, C. (1982). Interethnic Marriages. *International Journal of Comparative Sociology, 23*, 225.

Johnson, Ronald C., & Nagashi, Craig T. (1986). The Adjustment of Offspring of Within-Group and Interracial-Intercultural Marriages: A Comparison of Personality Factor Scores. *Journal of Marriage and the Family, 48*, 279.

Kelley, Michael Robert (1976). *Some Psychological and Sociological Factors Influencing Motivation for Interracial Marriage.* Doctoral Dissertation, California School of Professional Psychology.

Kitano, Harry H. L., Wai-Tsang, Lynn Chai, & Halanaka, Herbert (1984). Asian-American Interracial Marriage. *Journal of Marriage and the Family, 46*, 179.

Kreykamp, A. M. J., Schellevis, L., van Noort, L. G. A., & Kaptein, R. (1967). *Protestant-Catholic Marriages.* Philadelphia: The Westminster Press.

Kunkel, Mark A. (1990). Epectations About Counseling in Relation to Acculturation in Mexican-American and Anglo-American Student Samples. *Journal of Counseling Psychology, 37*, 286.

LaFromboise, Teresa D., Trimble, Joseph E., & Mohatt, Gerald V. (1990). Counseling Intervention and American Indian Tradition: An Integrative Approach. *The Counseling*

Psychologist 18 (4), 628-654.

The Last Taboo? (1991). *Ebony* 46:11, 74.

Lieberman, S., & Waters, M. (1985). Ethnic Mixtures in the United States. *Sociology and Social Research, 70,* 43.

Harris poll. *Life* (1971). Harris poll. Vol. 70, #20, page 66.

Lloyd, Arthur P. (1987). Multicultural Counseling: Does It Belong in a Counselor Education Program? *Counselor Education and Supervision, 26,* 164.

Locke, Don C. (1990). A Not So Provincial View of Multicultural Counseling. *Counselor Education and Supervision, 30,* 18-25.

Locke, Don C. (1981). Race, Identity, and Black Children: A Developmental Perspective. *Social Casework: The Journal of Contemporary Social Work, 62,* 53.

Logan, S. L. (1981). Race Identity and Black Children: A Developmental Prospective, Social Casework. *The Journal of Contemporary Social Work, 62,* 53.

Lowell, C. Stanley. (1962). *Protestant-Catholic Marriage.* Nashville: Broadman Press.

McDermott, J. F., Jr., & Maretzki, T. W. (Eds.). (1977). *Adjustment in Intercultural Marriage.* Honolulu: University of Hawaii Press.

McKenzie, Michael V. (1986). Ethnographic Findings on West Indian- American Clients. *Journal of Counseling and Development, 65,* 40.

McRoy, Ruth G., & Freeman, Edith. (1986). *Racial Identity Issues Among Mixed Race Children.* National Association of Social Workers.

Mace, David R. (1972). *Getting Ready for Marriage.* Nashville: Abington Press.

Methodist Church U.S.A. (1958). *The Pastor's Manual for Premarital Counseling*. Nashville: Methodist Publishing House.

Miles, Patrice, & Edwards, Audrey (1983). Black Women and White Men. *Essence, 14*, 94.

Monahan, Thomas P. (1976). The Occupation Class of Couples Entering into Interracial Marriages. *Journal of Comparative Family Studies, 7*, 175.

Morris, J. Kenneth (1960). *Premarital Counseling: A Manual for Ministers*. Englewood Cliffs, NJ: Prentice-Hall.

Murguia, Edward & Cazares, Ralph B. (1982). Intermarriage of Mexican Americans. *Marriage and Family Review 5*:91-100.

Newsweek (1984). Children of the Rainbow. Vol. 104, November 19, p. 120.

Norment, Lynn (1985). A Probing Look at Children of Interracial Marriage, *Ebony, 40*, 156.

Oates, Wayne E., & Rowatt, Wade (1975*). Before You Marry Them*. Nashville: Broadman Press.

O'Guinn, Thomas C., Imperia, Giovanna, & MacAdams, Elizabeth A. (1987). Acculturation and Perceived Family Decision-Making Input Among Mexican-American Wives. *Journal of Cross-Cultural Psychology, 18* (1), 7.

Parsonson, Karen (1987). Intermarriages: Effects on the Ethnic Identity of the Offspring. *Journal of Cross-Cultural Psychology, 18* (3), 363.

Payne, R. (1977). Racial Attitude Formation in Children of Mixed Black and White Heritage: Skin Color and Racial Identity. *Dissertation Abstracts International*. 38(6-B)2876.

Pastor's Manual for Premarital Counseling. (1958). Nashville: Methodist Publishing House.

Peca-Baker, Teresa, & Friedlander, Myrna L. (1987). Effects of Role Expectations on Clients' Perceptions of Disclosing and Non-Disclosing Counselors. *Journal of Counseling and Development, 66*, 78.

Pedersen, Paul (Ed.) (1985). *Handbook of Cross-Cultural Counseling and Therapy*. Westport, CT: Greenwood Press.

Pedersen, Paul (1987). Ten Frequent Assumptions of Cultural Bias in Counseling. *Journal of Multicultural Counseling and Development, 15* (1), 16-24.

Pike, James A. (1954). *If You Marry Outside Your Faith: Counsel on Mixed Marriages*. New York: Harper & Brothers.

Ponterotto, Joseph G. (1987). Counseling Mexican-Americans: A Multimodal Approach. *Journal of Counseling and Development, 65*, 308.

Porterfield, Ernest (1978). *Black and White Mixed Marriages: An Ethnographic Study of Black-White Families*. Chicago: Nelson Hall.

Poston, W. S. Carlos (1990). The Biracial Identity Model: A Needed Addition. *Journal of Counseling and Development, 69*, 152.

Poussaint, A. (1984). Study of Interracial Children Presents Positive Picture. *Interracial Books for Children*. Bull. 15:9-10.

Randolph, Laura B. (1989). Black Women/White Men: What's Goin' On? *Ebony, 44* (5), 154.

Rohrlich, Beulah F. (1988). Dual-Culture Marriage and Communication. *International Journal of Intercultural*

Relations, 12, 35.

Root, Maria P. P. (Ed.) (1992). *Racially Mixed People in America*. Newbury Park, NY: Sage Publications.

Rosser-Hogan, Ronda (1990). Making Counseling Culturally Appropriate: Intervention With a Montagnard Refugee. *Journal of Counseling and Development, 68*, 443.

Ruiz, Rene A., & Padilla, Amado M. (1977). Counseling Latinos. *Personnel and Guidance Journal, 55*, 401.

Rutledge, Aaron L. (1966). *Premarital Counseling*. Cambridge, MA: Schenman Publishing.

Sabnani, Haresh B., Ponterotto, Joseph G., & Borodovsky, Lisa G. (1991). White Racial Identity Development and Cross-Cultural Counselor Training: A Stage Model. *The Counseling Psychologist, 19* (1), 76.

Schlossberg, Nancy K. (Ed.). (1984). *Counseling Adults in Transition: Linking Practice with Theory*. New York: Springer Publishing.

SDA Church Manual (1976). Washington, D.C.: General Conference of Seventh-day Adventists.

Sebring, Deborah L. (1985). Considerations In Counseling Interracial Children. *Journal of Non-White Concerns, 13* (1), 3.

Secunda, Victona (1988). Marrying Out of Your Faith. *New Woman Magazine*.

Sherrow, Fred Solomon (1971). Patterns of Religious Intermarriage Among American College Graduates. Unpublished Doctoral Dissertation. New York: Columbia University.

Smart, Laura S. & Smart, Mollie S. (1980). *Families: Developing Relationships*. New York: MacMillian

Publishing.

Snider, Allan George (1971). *A Study of the Relationship Between Religious Affiliation, Religious Practices, and Marital Adjustment.* Unpublished Doctoral Dissertation, University of California, Los Angeles.

Simon, Paul & Simon, Jeanne (1967). *Protestant-Catholic Marriages Can Succeed.* New York: Association Press.

Smith, Elsie J. (1977). Counseling Black Individuals: Some Stereotypes. *Personnel and Guidance Journal, 55,* 390.

Stahmann, Robert F., & Hiebert, William J. (1980). *Premarital Counseling.* Lexington, MA: Lexington Books.

Stevens, G. (1985). Nativity, Intermarriage, and Mother-Tongue Shift. *American Sociological Review, 50,* 74.

Sue, Derald Wing (1981). *Counseling the Culturally Different: Theory and Practice.* New York: John Wiley & Sons.

Sweeting, M. (1969). *Les Eglises et Les Marriages Mixtes.* Paris: Les Editions Du Cerf.

Thelen, T. H. (1983). Minority Type Human Mate Preference. *Social Biology, 30,* 162.

Tiecher, J. (1968). Some Observations on Identity Problems in Children of Negro-White Marriages. *Journal of Nervous and Mental Disorders, 146,* 249.

Ting-Toomey, Stella (1991). Intimacy Expressions in Three Cultures: France, Japan, and the United States. *International Journal of Intercultural Relations, 15,* 29.

Triandis, Harry C., Lisanky, Judith, Setiadi, Bernadette, Chang, Bei-Hung, Marin, Gerardo, & Betancourt, Hector (1982). Stereotyping Among Hispanics and Anglos. *Journal of Cross-Cultural Psychology, 13* (4), 409.

Tseng, Wen-Shing, McDermott, John F., Jr., & Maretzki, Thomas W. (Eds.) (1977). *Adjustment on Intercultural Marriage*. Honolulu: University Press of Hawaii.

Tucker, M. Belinda, & Mitchell-Kernan, Claudia (1990). Black-American Intermarriage: The Social Structure. *Journal of Marriage and the Family, 52*, 209.

Turner, John N. (1982). Intermarriage and Assimilation in a Plural Society: Japanese-Americans in the United States. *Marriage and Family Review, 5*:61-73.

Vander Zanden, James W. (1979). *Sociology*. New York: John Wiley & Sons.

Veroff, Joseph (1989). Dimensions of Marital Well-being Among White and Black Newlyweds. *Journal of Marriage and the Family, 51* (2), 373.

Walton, H. (1962). Psychiatric Practice in a Multiracial Society. *Comparative Psychiatry, 3*, 265.

Washington, J. (1970). *Marriage in Black and White*. Boston: Beacon Press.

White, Ellen G. (1952). *The Adventist Home*. Nashville: Southern Publishing Association.

White, J. Gustav (1966). *When Your Advice Is Asked*. New York: A. J. Barnes.

Wilson, Barbara Foley (1984). Marriage's Melting Pot. *American Demographics, 6*:7, 34-37, 45.